Affordable to Build
HOME PLANS

GARLINGHOUSE

Library of Congress: 89-81343

ISBN: 0-938708-29-5

Canadian orders should be submitted to:

The Garlinghouse Company
20 Cedar Street North
Kitchener, Ontario N2H 2W8
(519) 743-4169

TABLE OF CONTENTS

Popular Home Designs
in Full Color 1-32
Home Plans
for Every Life Style 33-187
Blueprint Order Pages 188-189
Book Order Pages 190-192

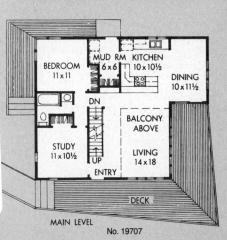

MAIN LEVEL   No. 19707

Value And Elegance Combined

D1567563

No. 19707

This design uses rough-finished wood on both exterior and interior walls, which saves labor and reduces maintenance later on. Tongue-and-groove decking over exposed joists substitutes for expensive floors and ceilings. The plan packs seven rooms, two baths, a dressing area, and a mud room into just two of the three floors. The lowest level, not shown, could easily be finished later. Floor-to-ceiling glass in the two-story living room produces a feeling of openness to the outside.

Main level—996 sq. ft.
Upper level—753 sq. ft.
Basement—900 sq. ft.

UPPER LEVEL

High Impact in a Small Package

No. 19491

From the sheltered veranda to the connected active areas, this award-winning home says "welcome." Look at the efficient U-shaped kitchen, with pass-through convenience that keeps the cook in the conversation around the dining table. Ceilings soar to dramatic heights in the adjoining living room. And, upstairs, the master loft with its own private deck provides a commanding view of the scene below, along with loads of built-in storage. With its own private bath and room-sized closet, this room will be a retreat you'll never want to leave. Tucked away from active areas, a roomy first-floor bedroom and study flank a combined bath and laundry center.

First floor – 920 sq. ft.
Second floor – 300 sq. ft.
Garage – 583 sq. ft.

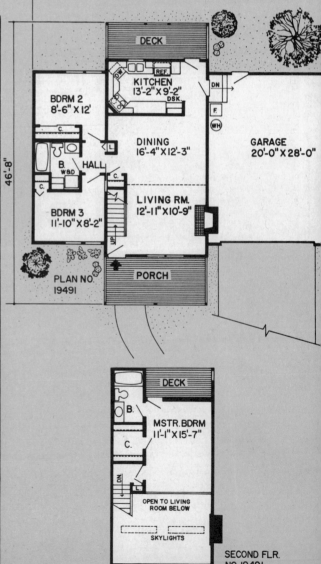

50'-0"

46'-8"

DECK

KITCHEN
13'-2" X 9'-2"

REF.

DW

DSK.

BDRM 2
8'-6" X 12'

C.

B.
W&D

HALL

C.

DINING
16'-4" X 12'-3"

DN

F

WH

GARAGE
20'-0" X 28'-0"

L

C.

BDRM 3
11'-10" X 8'-2"

LIVING RM.
12'-11" X 10'-9"

UP

PLAN NO.
19491

PORCH

DECK

B.

MSTR. BDRM
11'-1" X 15'-7"

C.

DN

OPEN TO LIVING
ROOM BELOW

SKYLIGHTS

SECOND FLR.
NO. 19491

Dramatic Energy Saver

No. 19915

Step inside this three-bedroom solar home, and you'll know why it won awards for its ingenious design. Twin greenhouses off living and family rooms provide dramatic views and a constant climate throughout the house. Giant cutouts and floor grates in the upstairs bedrooms insure a continuous flow of solar warmth. And, when the sun goes down, heat-holding brick floors and a massive fireplace will help keep the energy bills down. You'll appreciate the efficient galley kitchen that serves the dining room, family room, and outdoor deck with ease. Two full baths adjoin the bedrooms upstairs and down.

First floor – 1,218 sq. ft.
Second floor – 654 sq. ft.

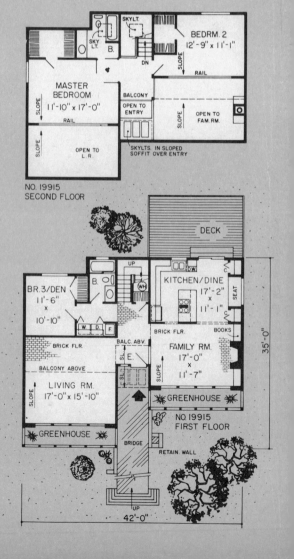

NO. 19915
SECOND FLOOR

NO. 19915
FIRST FLOOR

4

Flexibility Big Asset of Award-winning Design

No. 19938

This two-story home is ideal for those on a budget, yet looking for a design they can adapt to their needs as their budget allows. The primary living areas on the lower floor complete the basic one-bedroom, leaving the upper level, breezeway and garage for completion later, if necessary. The two rooms on the upper level could be used as bedrooms, a hobby room, private office, almost anything you choose. The family / dining / living areas are open to the multi-purpose room above and only partially divided from one another, creating a more spacious and formal atmosphere.

First floor—1,090 sq. ft.
Second floor—580 sq. ft.
Garage—484 sq. ft.

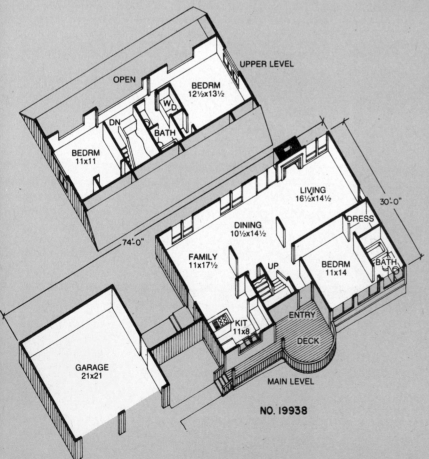

UPPER LEVEL

OPEN

BEDRM
12½x13½

W
D

DN

BATH

BEDRM
11x11

74'-0"

LIVING
16½x14½

DINING
10½x14½

DRESS

30'-0"

FAMILY
11x17½

UP

BEDRM
11x14

BATH

KIT
11x8

ENTRY

DECK

GARAGE
21x21

MAIN LEVEL

NO. 19938

Prize Winner

No. 19863

This cozy solar house took top prize in a nationwide design contest. Inside is a floor plan that's flexible enough to satisfy a wide variety of families and life-styles. The dominant feature of this passive solar system is the 32-foot-long greenhouse where the sun's heat is collected, stored and shared with the rest of the house, cutting energy bills in half. The house offers open spaces and partial ceilings to maximize airflow throughout.

First floor—1,000 sq. ft
Second floor—572 sq. ft.
Greenhouse—272 sq. ft.

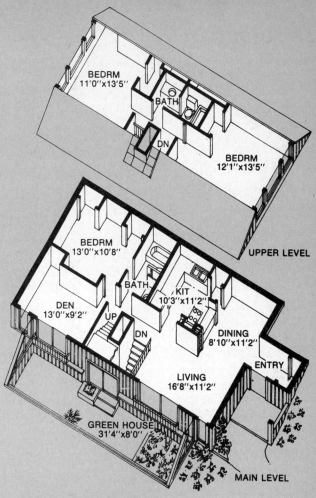

Wonderful Views Everywhere

No. 20068

Consider this home if your backyard is something special in each season. Both living and dining areas offer broad views across the deck to the beautiful scene beyond. Even the balcony on the second floor captures it all. The open floor plan in the interior of the home brings the view to the kitchen and front hall as well. The master bedroom, with a fabulous walk-in closet and lavish bath, maintains its privacy to the side while indulging in the view of the backyard. The second floor bedrooms are notable for the huge closets.

First floor — 1,266 sq. ft.
Second floor — 489 sq. ft.
Basement — 1,266 sq. ft.
Garage — 484 sq. ft.

A Karl Kreeger Design

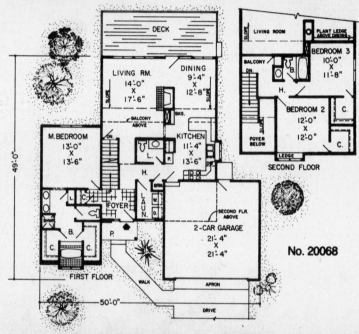

Elegant Entrance to Impressive Home

No. 20057

Two copper-roofed bay windows and a stone veneer front create an elegant entrance through an attractive circle head transom. Enjoy the vaulted ceilings that extend into the foyer, dining room, breakfast room, and master bedroom (with private dressing area). Even the kitchen is impressive with two separate eating areas and a connecting pantry for storage. Sliding glass doors from the breakfast room lead to a huge deck.

First floor — 1,804 sq. ft.
Basement — 1,804 sq. ft.
Garage & workshop — 499 sq. ft.

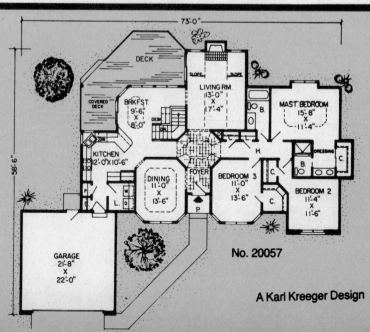

A Karl Kreeger Design

Family Comfort

No. 20129

From its Victorian-influenced exterior to its sloping, skylit hearth room with adjoining deck, this is a home with old-fashioned character. A double bump-out window adds sunlight and space to the first-floor master suite, which features a private bath with garden tub, double vanities, and dressing area. The living and dining rooms, separate yet open, span the entire width of the house. And the kitchen, just steps away, makes mealtime easy when you're entertaining. Step up the U-shaped staircase to two large bedrooms, each with a walk-in closet. A compartmentalized, second-floor bath features convenient double vanities you'll appreciate on busy mornings.

First floor — 1,593 sq. ft.
Second floor — 661 sq. ft.
Basement — 1,586 sq. ft.
Garage — 472 sq. ft.

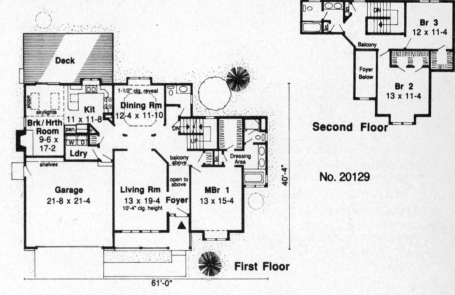

No. 20129

Second Floor

Br 3
12 x 11-4

Br 2
13 x 11-4

Balcony

Foyer
Below

Deck

Kit
11 x 11-8

Dining Rm
12-4 x 11-10

1-1/2" clg. reveal

Brk/Hrth
Room
9-6 x
17-2

pan.

W D

Ldry

shelves

Garage
21-8 x 21-4

Living Rm
13 x 19-4
10'-4" clg. height

Foyer

balcony
above

open to
above

DN

UP

Dressing
Area

MBr 1
13 x 15-4

40'-4"

61'-0"

First Floor

A Karl Kreeger Design

Formal Entry, Luxury Master Suite, Plus Room to Expand

No. 10525

In addition to the three, well-designed bedrooms, the second floor of this traditional design features a large unfinished area which could be a study, hobby center or even a fully-equipped exercise room. The luxury master suite has two walk-in closets in the dressing area plus a conveniently arranged five-piece bath which features a circular window above the tiled tub enclosure. The first floor is composed of formal dining and living rooms on either side of the tiled foyer with the family areas organized along the back overlooking the patio. The cozy family room has a fireplace, built-in bookcase and opens onto the patio. The kitchen features a bump-out window over sink and shares a snack bar with the bright and cheery breakfast nook.

First floor — 1,219 sq. ft.
Second floor — 1,010 sq. ft.
Basement — 1,219 sq. ft.
Garage — 514 sq. ft.

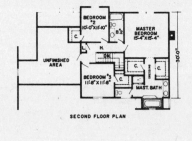

SECOND FLOOR PLAN

No. 10525

A Karl Kreeger Design

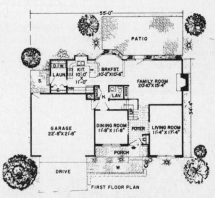

FIRST FLOOR PLAN

Carefully Designed for Compact Spaces

No. 10771

The amenities featured in this compact, one-level plan prove you don't have to build large to have what you want in a home. Notice the garden wall that insures privacy in the master suite, the two full baths, the attached garage, the built-in wetbar in the fireplaced living room, and the walled patio accessible through sliding glass doors in both dining and living rooms. Look at the mealtime choices you have: informal family suppers and quick snacks in the sunny breakfast nook, or elegant dinners in the spacious dining room overlooking the patio. Other assets of this appealing home include double closets and vanities in the master suite, and the handy laundry corner tucked off the breakfast room.

Main living area — 1,305 sq. ft.
Garage — one-car

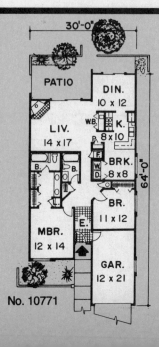

No. 10771

Inviting Porch Enlarges Compact Home

No. 10646

This modified Cape with attached two-car garage can house a growing family for a bargain price. Double doors in the cozy living room open to the bay-windowed family room with fireplace and patio access. Eat in the family-size kitchen or formal dining room. Up the central stairway, the vaulted ceiling in the master suite creates a spacious feeling. Three other bedrooms and a bath share the second floor.

First floor — 930 sq. ft.
Second floor — 980 sq. ft.
Basement — 900 sq. ft.
Garage — 484 sq. ft.

A Karl Kreeger Design

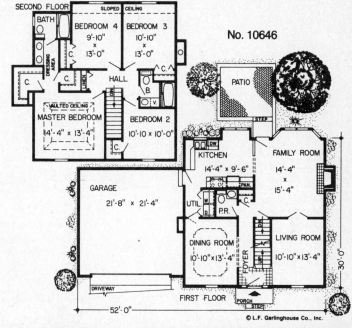

SECOND FLOOR

BATH

BEDROOM 4
9'-10"
x
13'-0"

SLOPED CEILING

BEDROOM 3
10'-10"
x
13'-0"

No. 10646

DRESSING AREA

C.

C.

HALL

LINEN

C.

B.

VAULTED CEILING

MASTER BEDROOM
14'-4" x 13'-4"

BEDROOM 2
10'-10 x 10'-0"

C.

PATIO
STEP

KITCHEN
14'-4" x 9'-6"

FAMILY ROOM
14'-4"
x
15'-4"

GARAGE
21'-8" x 21'-4"

UTIL

PAN.

W
D

P.R.

C.

DINING ROOM
10'-10" x 13'-4"

FOYER

LIVING ROOM
10'-10" x 13'-4"

30'-0"

DRIVEWAY

FIRST FLOOR

PORCH
STEP

52'-0"

© L.F. Garlinghouse Co., Inc.

Classic Farmhouse

No. 10362

This house says "home" to everyone who remembers the bygone era but thinks ahead for comfort and values. The big wrap porch follows tradition. Imagine the cool summer evenings spent there. A split landing stairway leads to the four bedrooms on the upper level, complete with two bathrooms and lots of closets, perfect for the growing family. On the main level a wood-burning, built-in fireplace in the living room adds to the nostalgic charm of this home. Sliding glass doors open onto the porch. The main level also boasts a den, lavatory, utility room, kitchen and separate dining room overlooking the porch. An enclosed breezeway connects the double garage to the house.

Main level — 1,104 sq. ft.
Upper level — 1,124 sq. ft.
Basement — 1,080 sq. ft.
Garage — 528 sq. ft.

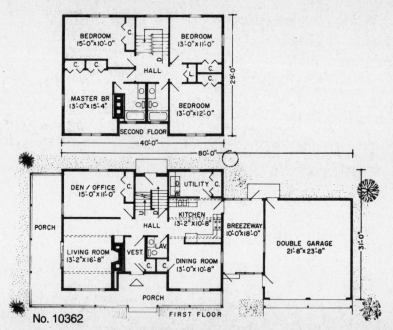

Railing Divides Living Spaces

No. 10596

This one-level design is a celebration of light and open space. From the foyer, view the dining room, island kitchen, breakfast room, living room, and outdoor deck in one sweeping glance. Bay windows add pleasing angles and lots of sunshine to eating areas and the master suite. And, a wall of windows brings the outdoors into the two back bedrooms.

Main living area — 1,740 sq. ft.
Basement — 1,377 sq. ft.
Garage — 480 sq. ft.

A Karl Kreeger Design

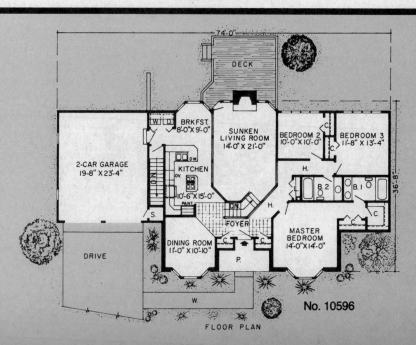

Clapboard Contemporary

No. 20367

It's hard to miss the focal point of this magnificent contemporary home; the window wall that graces the dramatic two-story living room is a feast for the eyes, inside and out. And the open plan of this three-bedroom beauty adds even more excitement to its spacious ambience. Eat in the dining room that adjoins the living room, or have a snack by the fire in the sunken family room overlooking the rear deck. The nearby kitchen is convenient to both. Bedrooms share the second floor with two full baths. Be sure to notice the unique balcony room off the master suite.

First floor — 996 sq. ft.
Second floor — 783 sq. ft.
Basement — 972 sq. ft.
Garage — 567 sq. ft.

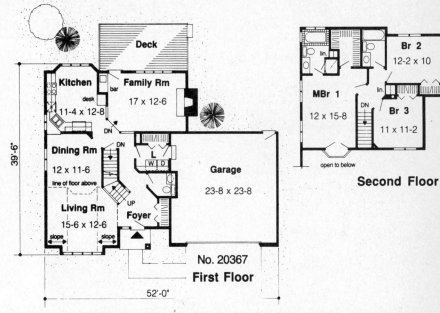

Deck

Kitchen
11-4 x 12-8
desk
bar

Family Rm
17 x 12-6

DN

Dining Rm
12 x 11-6
line of floor above
DN

W D

Living Rm
15-6 x 12-6
slope   slope
UP

Foyer

Garage
23-8 x 23-8

39'-6"

52'-0"

No. 20367
First Floor

Br 2
12-2 x 10

MBr 1
12 x 15-8

lin.

DN

Br 3
11 x 11-2

open to below

Second Floor

Sheltered Porch is an Inviting Entrance

No. 20070

Enjoy the beauty and tradition of a two-story home. From the spacious, tiled entry with coat closet to the seclusion of 2nd floor bedrooms, you'll appreciate the classic features that distinguish a two-story home. And you'll delight in the modern touches that make this plan sparkle: the handsome window treatment in the living room; the oversized master bedroom with walk-in closet and deluxe, skylit bath; the efficient kitchen and charming breakfast nook and the sweeping outdoor deck.

First floor — 877 sq. ft.
Second floor — 910 sq. ft.
Basement — 877 sq. ft.
Garage — 458 sq. ft.

A Karl Kreeger Design

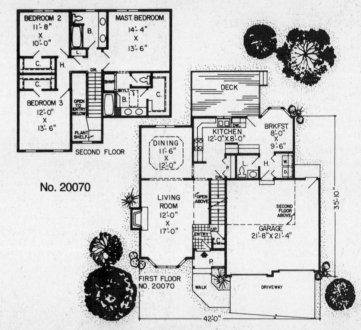

Wide-Open and Convenient

No. 20100

Stacked windows fill the wall in the front bedroom of this one-level home, creating an attractive facade, and a sunny atmosphere inside. Around the corner, two more bedrooms and two full baths complete the bedroom wing, set apart for bedtime quiet. Notice the elegant vaulted ceiling in the master bedroom, the master tub and shower illuminated by a skylight, and the double vanities in both baths. Active areas enjoy a spacious feeling. Look at the high, sloping ceilings in the fireplaced living room, the sliders that unite the breakfast room and kitchen with an adjoining deck, and the vaulted ceilings in the formal dining room off the foyer.

Main floor — 1,727 sq. ft.
Basement — 1,727 sq. ft.
Garage — 484 sq. ft.

A Karl Kreeger Design

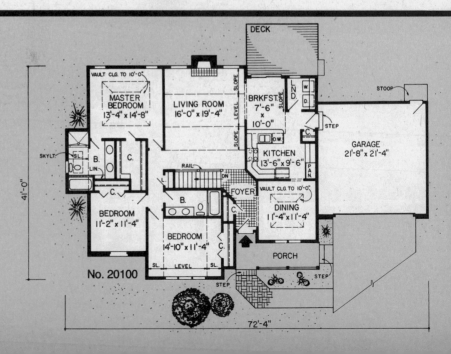

16

Sunny Character

No. 20158

From the welcoming porch to the balcony overlooking the skylit living room, this three bedroom beauty is loaded with sunny appeal. An elegant, bayed dining room adjoins the centrally located island kitchen, which features easy access to a screened porch. A short hall leads past the laundry and handy powder room to a huge, fireplaced living room that opens to a rear deck. Walk under the balcony to the first-floor master suite with its walk-in closet and luxury bath. You'll love the quiet, yet convenient location of this special retreat. The second floor balcony overlooking the living room and two-story foyer links two more bedrooms, each with a huge closet, and a large divided bath.

First floor — 1,293 sq. ft.
Second floor — 526 sq. ft.
Basement — 1,286 sq. ft.
Garage — 484 sq. ft.
Breezeway — 180 sq. ft.

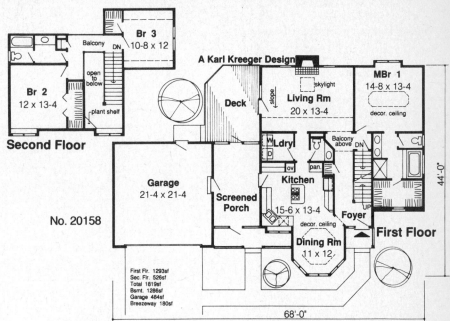

Second Floor

Br 3
10-8 x 12

Br 2
12 x 13-4

Balcony
DN

open to below

plant shelf

No. 20158

First Floor

A Karl Kreeger Design

Deck

Living Rm
20 x 13-4
skylight
slope
decor. ceiling

MBr 1
14-8 x 13-4
decor. ceiling

Ldry
W
D
ov
pan.

Balcony above
DN

Kitchen
15-6 x 13-4

Garage
21-4 x 21-4

Screened Porch

Foyer
UP

Dining Rm
11 x 12
decor. ceiling

First Flr. 1293sf
Sec. Flr. 526sf
Total 1819sf
Bsmt. 1286sf
Garage 484sf
Breezeway 180sf

68'-0"

44'-0"

Victorian Charm

No. 20366

The eaves of this splendid Victorian classic are perfect spots for covered porches: one to shelter the entry, and one for relaxing on a warm summer night. The central foyer divides the gathering room and formal dining room. To the rear, you'll find an island kitchen that opens to a sunny breakfast room overlooking a rear deck. A handy powder room and laundry room complete the main living area. The second floor possesses a character all its own, with a cozy window seat flanked by planters at the top of the stairs, a hall bath, built-in bookcases, and a walk-in closet for extra storage. Look at the luxurious master suite, with its private, oversized shower and garden spa, double vanities, and room-size closet.

First floor — 1,244 sq. ft.
Second floor — 1,100 sq. ft.

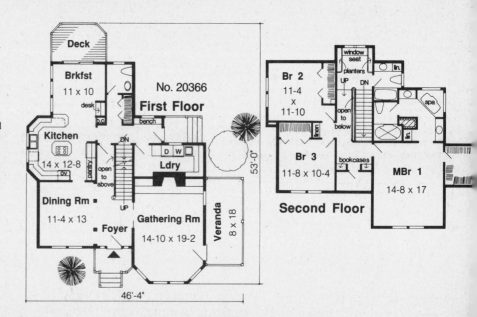

Cathedral Window Graced by Massive Arch

No. 20066

A tiled threshold provides a distinctive entrance into this spacious home. There's room for gracious living everywhere, from the comfortable living room with a wood-burning fireplace and tiled hearth, to the elegant dining room with a vaulted ceiling, to the outside deck. Plan your meals in a kitchen that has all the right ingredients: a central work island, pantry, planning desk, and breakfast area. A decorative ceiling will delight your eye in the master suite, which includes a full bath and bow window.

First floor — 1,850 sq. ft.
Basement — 1,850 sq. ft.
Garage — 503 sq. ft.

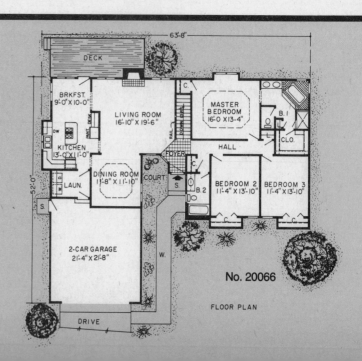

A Karl Kreeger Design

Sunny and Spacious

No. 20302

The wood detailing that radiates from the half round window of this inviting family home hints at the sunny atmosphere you'll find inside. Walking through the vestibule past the formal and family dining rooms, you'll encounter a two-way fireplace that warms the living and family rooms at the rear of the house. Notice the double sliders that link both rooms to a massive rear deck, and the pass-through convenience afforded by the U-shaped kitchen. Tucked behind the garage for privacy, the first-floor master suite features a skylit bath with double vanities and a luxurious spa tub. And, upstairs, three bedrooms open to a skylit lounge with a bird's eye view of the family room.

First floor — 1,510 sq. ft.
Second floor — 820 sq. ft.
Basement — 1,284 sq. ft.
Garage — 430 sq. ft.

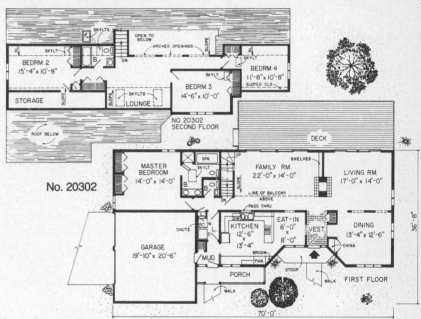

No. 20302

Classic Charm

No. 20157

Choose this home if you're looking for an up-to-date plan with the old-fashioned romance of Victorian architecture. You'll feel the spacious atmosphere that pervades this special home the moment you walk into the two-story foyer. A formal dining room with elegant bay windows and decorative ceilings is mirrored in the tower bedroom upstairs. The well-appointed kitchen easily serves both the dining room and the sunny hearth room overlooking the deck. A two-way fireplace separates this cozy spot from the dramatic, soaring living room. The front and rear bedroom upstairs share a full-hall bath, but the master suite enjoys its own private bath, along with a room-sized closet brightened by a bump-out window.

First floor — 1,086 sq. ft.
Second floor — 937 sq. ft.
Basement — 1,086 sq. ft.
Garage — 490 sq. ft.

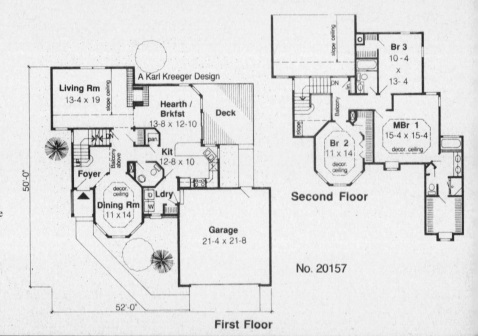

Simple Lines Enhanced by Elegant Window Treatment

No. 10503

Consider this plan if you work at home and would enjoy a homey, well lit office or den. The huge, arched window floods the front room with light. This house offers a lot of other practical details for the two-career family. Compact and efficient use of space means less to clean and organize. Yet the open plan keeps the home from feeling too small and cramped. Other features like plenty of closet space, step-saving laundry facilities, easily-cleaned kitchen, and window wall in the living room make this a delightful plan.

First floor — 1,486 sq. ft.
Garage — 462 sq. ft.
Basement — 1,486 sq. ft.

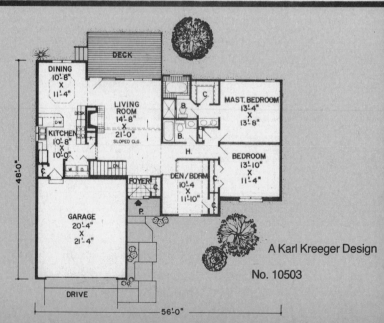

Enjoy a Crackling Fire on a Chilly Day

No. 10683

From the dramatic, two-story entry to the full-length deck off the massive great room, this is a modern plan in a classic package. Cathedral ceilings soar over the formal dining and sunken living rooms, separated by an open railing. The corner kitchen efficiently serves formal and family eating areas. Can't you imagine a table overlooking the deck in the sunken great room's sunny bay? Up the angular staircase, two bedrooms, each with a huge closet, share a full bath. You'll have your own, private bath, including double vanities and a sun-washed raised tub, in the master suite at the rear of the house.

First floor — 990 sq. ft.
Second floor — 721 sq. ft.
Basement — 934 sq. ft.
Garage — 429 sq. ft.

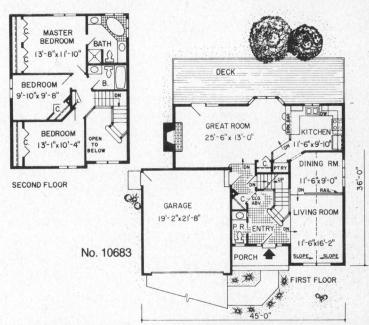

Colonial Character

No. 20136

A traditional exterior combines with a terrific, open plan in this updated Colonial classic. The formal parlor and dining room flanking the central foyer are loaded with old-fashioned charm. Step back to the living room for an exciting surprise, where decorative beams accentuate the sloping ceiling it shares with the breakfast room overlooking the deck. Separated from the adjoining kitchen by a half wall and warmed by a fireplace, this is a spacious, yet cozy area your family will enjoy for years. You'll appreciate the private, first floor master suite, which features its own, double-vanitied bath. Tuck the kids in upstairs, where two bedrooms share a skylit bath and loads of closet space.

First floor — 1,556 sq. ft.
Second floor — 539 sq. ft.
Basement — 1,556 sq. ft.
Garage — 572 sq. ft.

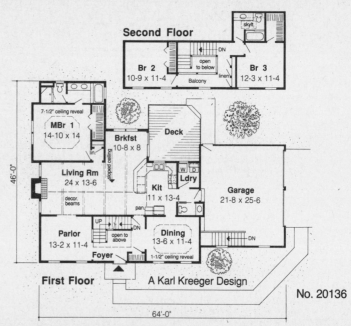

Bedrooms Flank Active Areas for Privacy

No. 20104

Hate to climb stairs? This one-level gem will accommodate your family in style, and keep your housework to a minimum. Recessed ceilings add an elegant touch to the dining room and master suite. And, with half walls, skylights, and a handy rear deck off the sunny breakfast room, there's an airy feeling throughout the centrally-located active areas. You'll appreciate the convenience of built-in storage in the kitchen and fireplaced living room, and the huge bedroom closets that keep the clutter down. Look at the private master bath with its twin vanities, raised tub and walk-in shower. Don't you deserve a little luxury?

Main living area — 1,686 sq. ft.
Basement — 1,677 sq. ft.
Garage — 475 sq. ft.

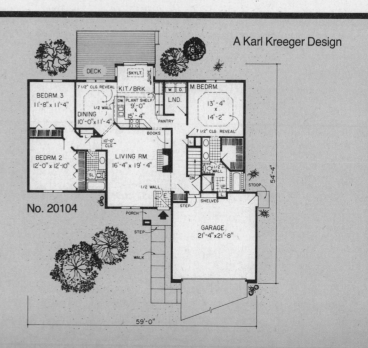

Two-Story Window Flanked By Stone Dominates Facade

No. 10494

The tiled foyer conveniently leads to the upper two bedrooms, the master bedroom, and the central living room. A corner built-in bookcase, fireplace and dramatic window wall complete this gracious room. The front dining room, enhanced by natural lighting, is convenient to the kitchen and adjacent breakfast nook.

First floor — 1,584 sq. ft.
Second floor — 599 sq. ft.
Basement — 1,584 sq. ft.
Garage — 514 sq. ft.

A Karl Kreeger Design

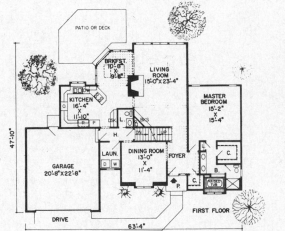

No. 10494

Open Plan Accented by Loft, Windows and Decks

No. 10515

The first floor living space of this inviting home blends the family room and dining room for comfortable family living. The large kitchen shares a preparation-eating bar with the dining room. The ample utility room is designed with a pantry, plus room for a freezer, washer and dryer. Also on the first floor is the master suite with its two closets and five piece bath which opens into a greenhouse. The second floor is highlighted by a loft which overlooks the first floor living area. The two upstairs bedrooms each have double closets and share a four-piece, compartmentalized bath.

First floor — 1,280 sq. ft.
Second floor — 735 sq. ft.
Greenhouse — 80 sq. ft.
Playhouse — 80 sq. ft.

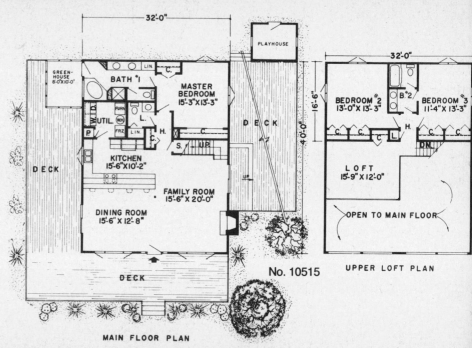

No. 10515

UPPER LOFT PLAN

MAIN FLOOR PLAN

Facade Features Vertical Columns

No. 10645

This two-story home is perfect for the family that wants to keep sleeping quarters quiet. Closets and a hallway muffle sound from the foyer. Upstairs, the location of two additional bedrooms and full skylit bath over the garage and sleeping areas below insures a restful atmosphere. The dining room is located directly off the foyer. With an angular ceiling and massive fireplace, the great room opens to the kitchen and breakfast nook, which features sliding glass doors to an outdoor patio.

First floor — 1,628 sq. ft.
Second floor — 609 sq. ft.
Basement — 1,616 sq. ft.
Garage — 450 sq. ft.

A Karl Kreeger Design

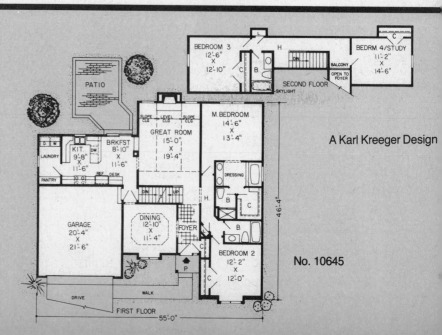

No. 10645

FIRST FLOOR

Farmhouse Flavor

No. 10785

The charm of an old fashioned farmhouse combines with sizzling contemporary excitement in this three-bedroom home. Classic touches abound, from the clapboard exterior with its inviting, wrap-around porch to the wood stove that warms the entire house. Inside, the two-story foyer, crowned by a plant ledge high overhead, affords a view of the soaring, skylit living room and rear deck beyond sliding glass doors. To the right, there's a formal dining room with bay window, just steps away from the kitchen. The well-appointed master suite completes the first floor. Upstairs, you'll find a full bath and two more bedrooms, each with a walk-in closet and cozy gable sitting nook.

First floor — 1,269 sq. ft.
Second floor — 638 sq. ft.
Basement — 1,269 sq. ft.

Second Floor

slope
skylight
open to below
Balcony
slope
Br 2
10-4 x 14
DN
Br 3
11 x 14
plant ledge
slope

Deck
Living Rm
13 x 19-6
pan
W D
Ldry
MBr 1
13-6 x 14
wood stove
Kitchen
11 x 12
DN
Dining Rm
12-10 x 13-6
Foyer
39'-0"
47'-0"

No. 10785
First Floor

Porch Adorns Elegant Bay

No. 20093

Here's a compact Victorian charmer that unites tradition with today in a perfect combination. Imagine waking up in the roomy master suite with its romantic bay and full bath with double sinks. Two additional bedrooms, which feature huge closets, share the hall bath. The romance continues in the sunny breakfast room off the island kitchen, in the recessed ceilings of the formal dining room, and in the living room's cozy fireplace. Sun lovers will appreciate the sloping, skylit ceilings in the living room, and the rear deck accessible from both the kitchen and living room.

First floor — 1,027 sq. ft.
Second floor — 812 sq. ft.
Basement — 978 sq. ft.
Garage — 484 sq. ft.

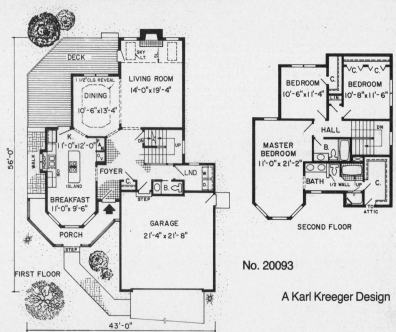

No. 20093

A Karl Kreeger Design

Two-Way Fireplace Warms Living Areas

No. 10652

Stucco, fieldstone, and rough-hewn timbers grace the elegant exterior of this three-bedroom family home. But with abundant windows, high ceilings, and an open plan, this cheerful abode is a far cry from the chilly tudor castle of long ago. Flanked by a vaulted formal dining room and a stairway to the upstairs bedrooms, full bath, and built-in cedar closet, the central foyer leads to a spacious living room, kept comfortable in any season by a ceiling fan. Nearby, the first-floor master suite is loaded with amenities: a walk-in closet, skylit double vanities, and a sunken tub. Notice the cooktop island convenience in the kitchen, the built-in bar adjacent to the living room, and the rear deck accessible through French doors in the breakfast room.

First floor — 1,789 sq. ft.
Second floor — 568 sq. ft.
Basement — 1,789 sq. ft.
Garage — 529 sq. ft.

No. 10652

A Karl Kreeger Design

Multi-Level Excitement

No. 20102

With abundant windows, a skylit breakfast room with sliders to a rear deck, and an open plan over-looking the sunken living room below, the foyer level of this distinctive home is a celebration of open space. You'll appreciate the step-saving design of the island kitchen that easily serves both dining rooms. And, you'll enjoy the warmth of the living room fireplace throughout the lower levels of the house. A stairway leads from the foyer to the bedroom level that houses the spacious master suite with a private bath, and two additional bedrooms served by a full bath. The lucky inhabitant of the fourth bedroom, tucked away at the top of the house, will love this private retreat overlooking the two floors below.

First level — 1,003 sq. ft.
Second level — 808 sq. ft.
Third level — 241 sq. ft.
Basement — 573 sq. ft.
Garage — 493 sq. ft.

No. 20102

A Karl Kreeger Design

One-Floor Living, Tudor Style

No. 20099

You'll find an appealing quality of open space in every room of this unique one-level home. Angular windows and recessed ceilings separate the two dining rooms from the adjoining island kitchen without compromising the airy feeling. A window-wall that flanks the fireplace in the soaring, skylit living room unites interior spaces with the outdoor deck. The sunny atmosphere continues in the master suite, with its bump-out window and double-vanitied bath, and in the two bedrooms off the foyer.

First floor — 2,020 sq. ft.
Basement — 2,020 sq. ft.
Garage — 534 sq. ft.

A Karl Kreeger Design

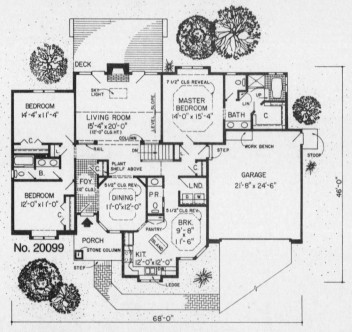

Compact Comfort

No. 10787

With its abundant windows and open plan, this sunny home will be warm and bright even on a chilly day. Soaring ceilings and a wall of stacked windows add dramatic volume to the spacious living room off the large central foyer. A step down, past the open railing, the dining room completes the formal area of the house so perfect for entertaining. For informal gatherings, walk into the kitchen-family room combination, separated by a handy breakfast bar. A cozy fireplace with wood storage and a built-in entertainment center combine with the efficient kitchen layout for a comfortable, convenient family area. Upstairs, you'll find three bedrooms and two full baths, including the luxury bath in the master suite.

First floor — 1,064 sq. ft.
Second floor — 708 sq. ft.
Basement — 1,064 sq. ft.
Garage — 576 sq. ft.

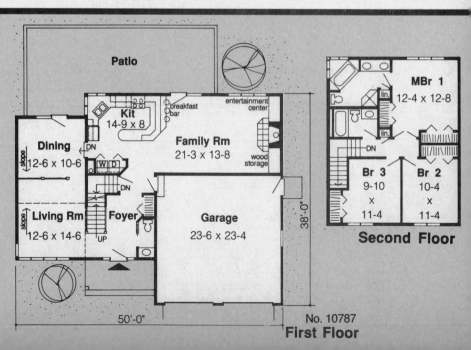

Carefree Living on One Level

No. 20089

Here's an inviting little charmer that will keep house-work to a minimum and give you plenty of room for hobbies. A full basement and oversized two-car garage is large enough to store your cars and boat, with space left for a workshop. Upstairs, one-level living is a breeze in this plan that keeps active and quiet areas separate. Three bedrooms and two full baths tucked down a hallway include the spacious master suite with double vanities. The fireplaced living room, dining room, and kitchen are wide open and conveniently arranged for easy mealtimes. Take it easy after dinner, and enjoy dessert and cof-fee outside on the deck off the dining room.

Main living area — 1,588 sq. ft.
Basement — 780 sq. ft.
Garage — 808 sq. ft.

A Karl Kreeger Design

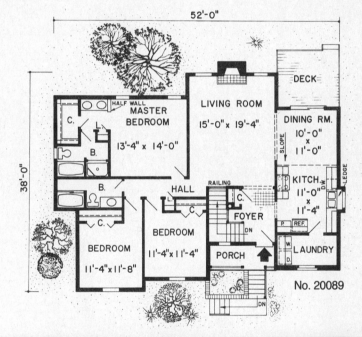

No. 20089

A Classic Family Treasure

No. 20357

Picture yourself in the beautiful surroundings of this compact, traditional Victorian. Bay windows add a light and airy feeling to the spacious, fireplaced living room and convenient island kitchen. Enjoy elegant suppers in the dining room overlooking the rear yard, or informal family meals in the cozy breakfast nook. The rear deck off the dining room makes eating outdoors a pleasant, warm-weather option. The handy powder room near the laundry is a convenience you'll surely appreciate. The traditional plan continues upstairs in the bayed master suite with double closets and private bath with step-in shower. A full bath serves the other two bedrooms on the second floor.

First floor — 910 sq. ft.
Second floor — 798 sq. ft.
Basement — 910 sq. ft.
Garage — 528 sq. ft.

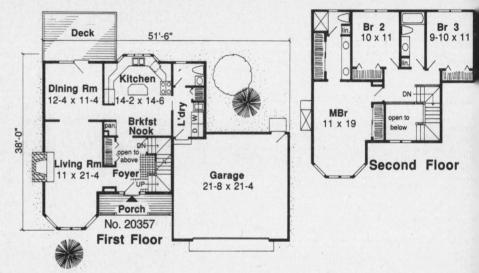

Stunning Split-Entry

No. 20143

This spacious split-entry home with a contemporary flavor is the perfect answer to the needs of your growing family. Imagine the convenience of a rec room with a built-in bar, powder room, and storage space on the garage level. Picture the luxury of your own, private master suite tucked off the foyer, featuring a walk-in closet, double-vanitied bath, and decorative ceilings. Active areas a few steps up include an expansive, fireplaced living room over-looking the foyer, an adjoining dining room graced with decorative ceilings and columns, and a skylit kitchen and breakfast room loaded with built-in amenities. Two bedrooms over the garage are steps away from the hall bath or the powder room.

Upper floor — 1,599 sq. ft.
Lower floor — 346 sq. ft.
Garage — 520 sq. ft.

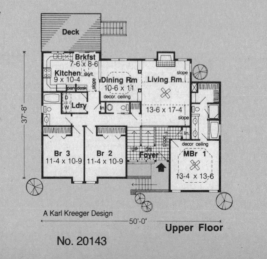

A Karl Kreeger Design

No. 20143

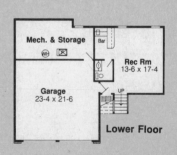

Classic Drama

No. 20165

The traditional clapboard exterior of this tidy home is deceiving. Step inside and you'll find drama on a grand scale. The central foyer, crowned by a balcony, slopes upward to meet the high ceilings of the fireplaced living room. At the rear of the house, you'll find a skylit dining room with a three-sided view of the adjoining deck. Just across the counter, the gourmet kitchen features a built-in desk and loads of cabinets. Three bedrooms share the second floor with two full baths. Rear bedrooms share the hall bath, but the master suite boasts a luxury bath complete with double vanities and a garden tub. Notice the generous closet and storage space throughout this exceptional, compact home.

First floor — 901 sq. ft.
Second floor — 864 sq. ft.
Basement — 901 sq. ft.
Garage — 594 sq. ft.

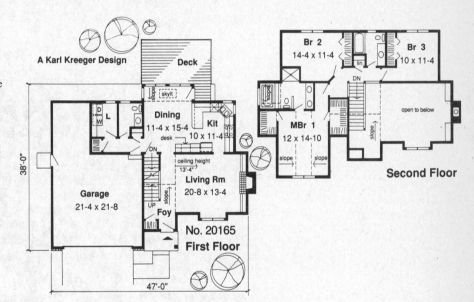

A Karl Kreeger Design

Deck

Dining
11-4 x 15-4

Kit
10 x 11-4

desk

ceiling height
13'-4"

Living Rm
20-8 x 13-4

Garage
21-4 x 21-8

Foy

UP

DN

38'-0"

47'-0"

No. 20165
First Floor

Br 2
14-4 x 11-4

Br 3
10 x 11-4

DN

MBr 1
12 x 14-10

open to below

slope

Second Floor

Stucco and Stone Reveal Outstanding Tudor Design

No. 10555

This beautiful stucco and stone masonry Tudor design opens to a formal foyer that leads through double doors into a well-designed library which is also conveniently accessible from the master bedroom. The master bedroom offers a vaulted ceiling and a huge bath area. Other features are an oversized living room with a fireplace, an open kitchen and a connecting dining room. A utility room and half bath are located next to a two-car garage. One other select option in this design is the separate cedar closet to use for off-season clothes storage.

First floor — 1,671 sq. ft.
Second floor — 505 sq. ft.
Basement — 1,661 sq. ft.
Garage — 604 sq. ft.
Screened porch — 114 sq. ft.

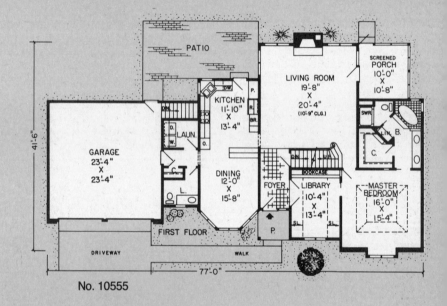

No. 10555

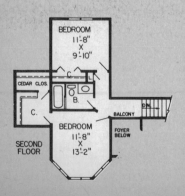

Elegant Master Suite Crowns Victorian

No. 20351

Gingerbread trim, round-top windows, and a two-story bay window bring a Victorian flavor to this modern plan. A fireplace adds a cozy charm to the angular living room just off the foyer. Walk past the stairs and the handy powder room to the rear of the house. Flanked by the formal dining and family rooms, the convenient kitchen lets the cook enjoy family activities and prepare dinner, too! You'll appreciate the outdoor living space the rear deck adds. But, when there's a chill in the air, you can light a fire and enjoy the view from the window seat in the family room. Three upstairs bedrooms include the bayed master suite, which features loads of closet space, a raised whirlpool tub, and a step-in shower for busy mornings.

First floor — 1,304 sq. ft.
Second floor — 1,009 sq. ft.
Basement — 1,304 sq. ft.
Garage — 688 sq. ft.

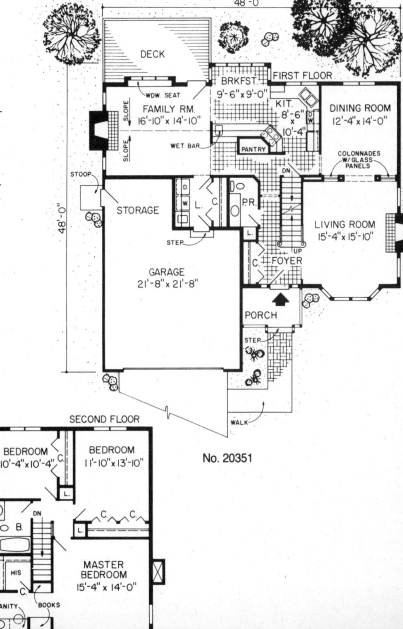

No. 20351

Design Portrays Expensive Look

No. 90040

Inside the front entrance and beyond the foyer, a square reception hall divides traffic to either living or service area. Located here is a powder room for easy guest use. To the left the 20 x 13 living room with its 8-foot wide bank of front windows, log burning fireplace and French doors to the connecting porch provides adequate, comfortable space for three-bedroom living. Their use will continue to be appreciated over the years of the day-to-day living. The curving staircase to the second floor leads to the sleeping level. To the right is a large storage area. A space to the rear could, by day, be finished as a den or office which still would leave plenty of storage. Two baths offer more than adequate service for the three bedrooms. A round master bath is located in the turret.

First floor — 1,069 sq. ft.
Second floor — 948 sq. ft.

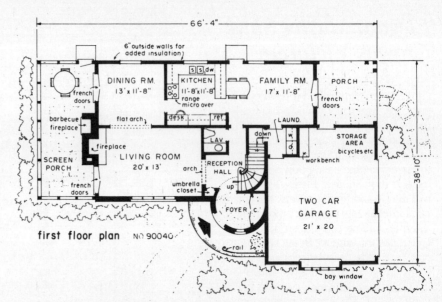

first floor plan   NO 90040

No. 90040

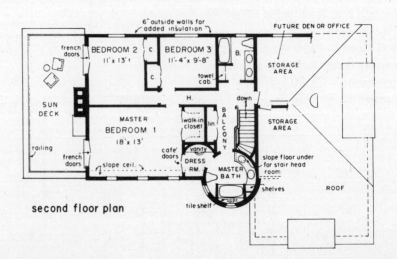

second floor plan

A Modern Plan with a Farmhouse Flavor

No. 90201

Here's a four-bedroom gem touched with the charm of another era. Yesterday's features include the sprawling covered porch, a cozy family room warmed by a raised-hearth fireplace, and a formal din-ing room with a large bay window. Huge windows, French doors, and sliding glass doors bring a sunny ambiance to every corner of this beautiful home. The open arrangement of formal and family areas add a spacious feeling you'll surely appreciate. Notice the handy kitchen built-ins, and the extra storage space by the garage entry and in the huge, third-floor attic. Upstairs, you'll find four bed-rooms and two full baths.

First floor — 1,370 sq. ft.
Second floor — 969 sq. ft.
Garage — 2-car

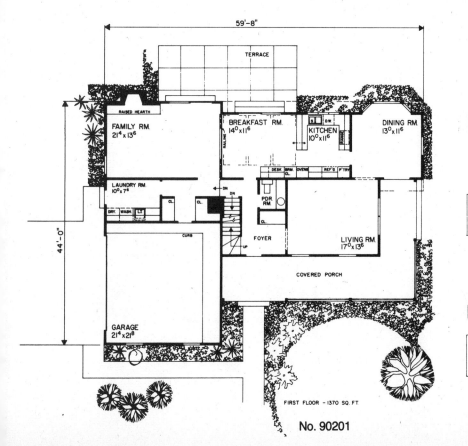

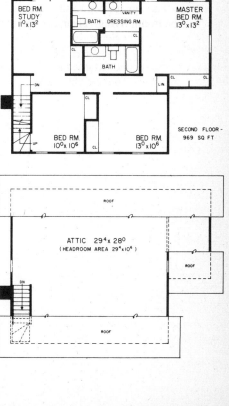

Arched Window Graces Formal Living Room

No. 90910

Lots of attention to fine detail sets this family jewel apart from the average house. An unusual, attractive porch shelters your arrival. Inside, open spaces, soaring ceilings, and a well-placed skylight provide a wonderful feeling of spaciousness. The excellent traffic pattern and zoning of this design will make living here a delight. Up the open staircase you will find three large bedrooms with many other special features. A whirlpool and make-up vanity in the master suite, double sinks in the family bath, and a knock-out window perfect for curling up with a favorite book will add to your enjoyment.

Main floor — 1,099 sq. ft.
Second floor — 846 sq. ft.
Garage — 483 sq. ft.
Width — 42 ft.
Depth — 44 ft.

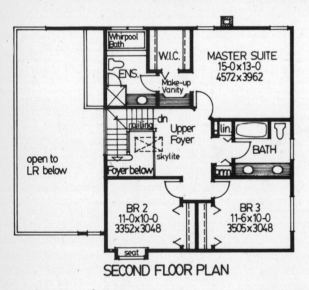

SECOND FLOOR PLAN

No. 90910

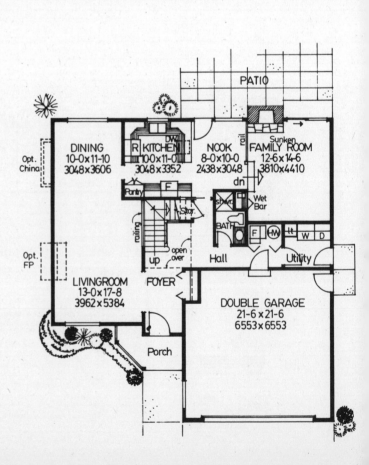

Deck Surrounds
House on Three Sides

No. 91304

Sitting in the sunken, circular living room of this elegant family home, you'll feel like you're outdoors even when you're not. Windows on four sides combine with a vaulted clerestory for a wide-open feeling you'll love year-round.

When it's warm, throw open the windows, or relax on the deck. But, when there's a chill in the air, back-to-back fireplaces keep the atmosphere toasty in the living room and adjoining great room. Even the convenient kitchen, with its bay dining nook, enjoys a back yard view. Do you sew? You'll love this roomy spot just steps away from the kitchen. Bump-out and bay windows give the three upstairs bedrooms a cheerful atmosphere, and cozy sitting nooks.

First floor — 1,372 sq. ft.
Second floor — 858 sq. ft.

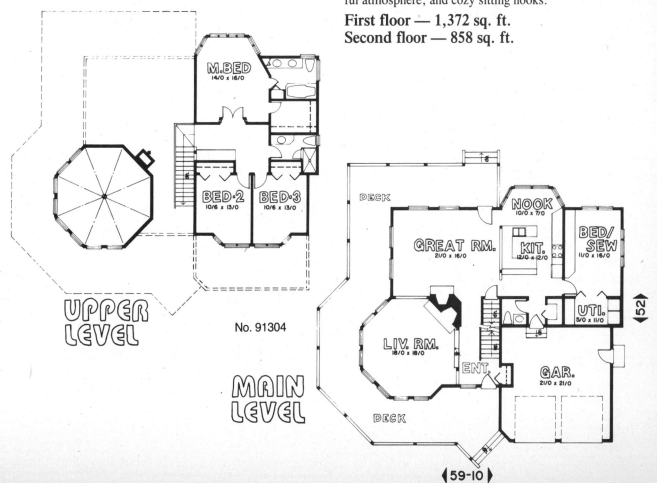

UPPER LEVEL

No. 91304

MAIN LEVEL

59-10

Open Floor Plan Enhances Home

No. 90307

The fireside room of this unique plan features a built-in sofa and opens onto both the kitchen and the dining room. Enclosed in glass and featuring the fireplace for which it is named, this room is designed to be the focal point of the home. The one-walled kitchen and its island are centrally located to accommodate any number of activities. The entry deck and the patio area off the dining room provide facilities for informal meals or outdoor parties. The single bedroom is located on the second level and incorporates its own bump-out window to fill with plants. An inviting sitting room completes this compact plan.

Total area — 1,152 sq. ft.

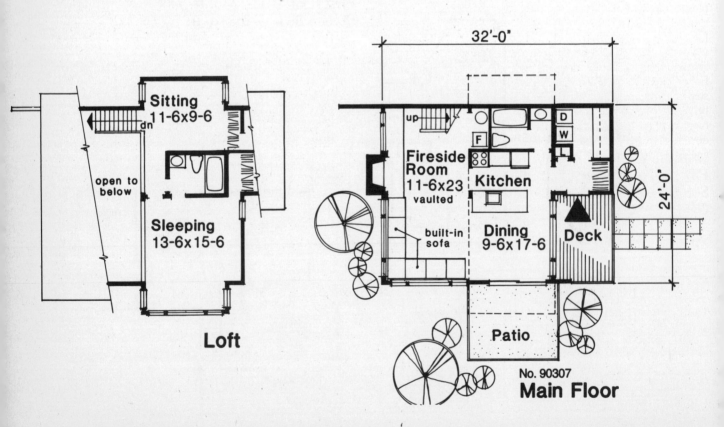

Sitting
11-6x9-6

open to below

Sleeping
13-6x15-6

Loft

32'-0"

up

Fireside Room
11-6x23
vaulted

Kitchen

built-in sofa

Dining
9-6x17-6

Deck

24'-0"

Patio

No. 90307
Main Floor

Impressive, Inside and Out

No. 99301

With its tall expanses of glass and towering gables, this three bedroom beauty is loaded with curbside appeal. But the interior sizzles with the excitement of a two-story stairwell flanked by a vaulted, sunken living room and elegant dining room. Romantic but functional French doors divide formal and family areas, a plus when you're entertaining. The sunny breakfast bay divides the efficient kitchen from the sunken family room, which features built-in bookcases, a massive fireplace, and easy patio access. Enjoy the view of the living room as you step up the open staircase to three ample bedrooms. Be sure to notice the sumptuous master suite, with its bay-windowed bath, corner window treatments, and room-sized closet.

First floor — 1,288 sq. ft.
Second floor — 910 sq. ft.
Garage — 2-car

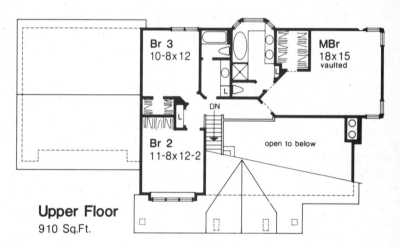

Upper Floor
910 Sq.Ft.

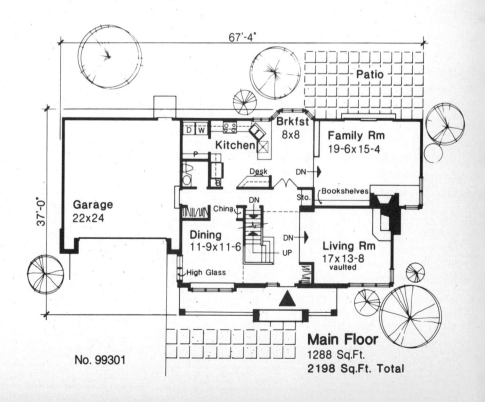

No. 99301

Main Floor
1288 Sq.Ft.
2198 Sq.Ft. Total

Bow Window Creates Striking Living Room

No. 9310

This split-foyer design has a very attractive facade which includes a large bow window in the living room and two square bay windows in the front bedrooms. The efficient kitchen joins the dining area for direct access to the rear deck. The lower level includes a large recreation room, utility room, and a workshop.

Upper level — 1,461 sq. ft.
Lower level — 740 sq. ft.
Garage and workshop — 651 sq. ft.

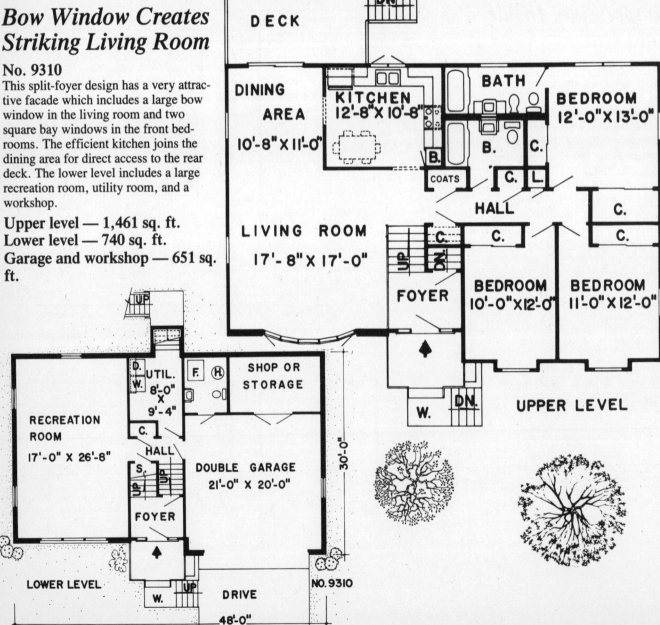

Above Reproach

No. 91002

Perched above an uneven lot, this house transforms an awkward site to greet and impress your family and guests. The welcome continues inside where the firedrum fireplace warms both entryway and living room. Both living and dining rooms open out onto a deck that surrounds the house on three sides. The downstairs bedroom has its own bath, and the enclosed sleeping room with two bunk beds is adjacent to a loft large enough to be divided. The second full bath provides for a large group of guests. If you don't love company, watch out. Your company will love your home.

Main Level — 744 sq. ft.
Upper Level — 288 sq. ft.

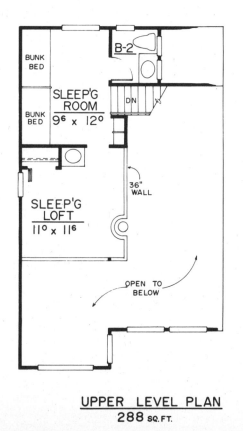

BUNK BED

B-2

SLEEP'G ROOM
9^6 x 12^0

DN

SLEEP'G LOFT
11^0 x 11^6

36" WALL

OPEN TO BELOW

UPPER LEVEL PLAN
288 SQ. FT.

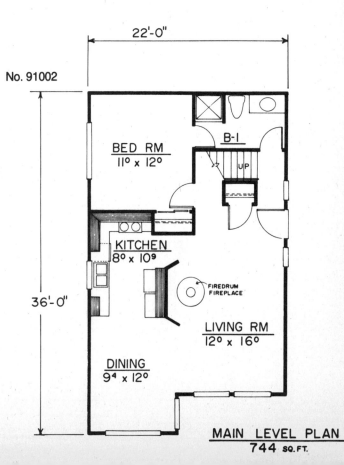

No. 91002

22'-0"

BED RM
11^0 x 12^0

B-1

UP

KITCHEN
8^0 x 10^9

FIREDRUM FIREPLACE

36'-0"

LIVING RM
12^0 x 16^0

DINING
9^4 x 12^0

MAIN LEVEL PLAN
744 SQ. FT.

Open, Yet Cozy Contemporary Cuts Housework

No. 90236

Do you hate housework? You'll breeze through this easy-care contemporary, leaving you plenty of time to relax on the rear terrace accessible from both the gathering and dining rooms. This modern gem features a wide-open main floor with plenty of storage space, an efficient kitchen, and a powder room by the handy garage entry. The study off the foyer could double as a guest room or home office. The U-shaped stairs lead to three bedrooms, each including huge closets to keep clutter to a minimum. Want to get away by yourself? Retire to your private balcony off the master suite.

First floor — 975 sq. ft.
Second floor — 1,024 sq. ft.
Garage — 2-car

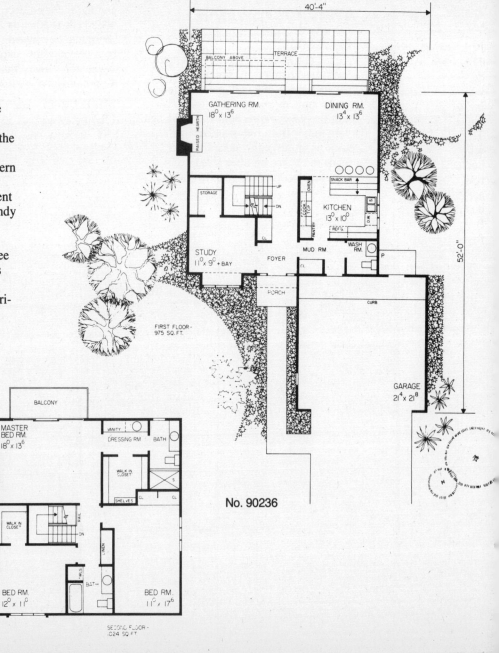

Stately Tudor

No. 90002

This imposing and impressive facade was designed to satisfy the scrutiny of those who love English details. The eye-catching tower soars above the main roof, housing a dramatic interior stair foyer. The tower is further enhanced by a bay window, shed roofs, dormers, open timber work, and truncated, gabled, and hip roofs. The carved double-entrance doors are flanked by iron grilled side lights. A dual closet vestibule greets guests and flows into a 11 x 13 ft. curved-stair foyer. The living room is large and

impressive with its 9 foot high window, 7 foot wide window seat, log burning fireplace with 13 foot hearth, and double French doors leading to the rear porch.

First floor — 1,679 sq. ft.
Second floor — 1,040 sq. ft.

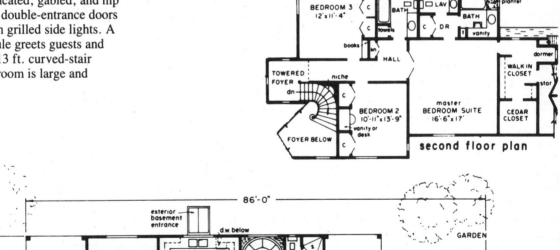

second floor plan

first floor plan

No. 90002

Country Kitchen and Great Room

No. 90419

Front porch, dormers, shutters and multi-paned windows on the exterior of this Cape Cod design are complimented by an informal interior. The main floor is divided into three sections. In the first section is an eat-in country kitchen with island counter and bay window and a large utility room which can be entered from either the kitchen or garage. The second section is the great room with inside fireplace, an informal dining nook and double doors opening onto the rear deck. The master suite features a walk-in closet and compartmentalized bath with linen closet. The upper floor consists of a second full bath and two bedrooms with ample closet space and window seats. A large storage area is provided over the garage.

First floor — 1,318 sq. ft.
Second floor — 718 sq. ft.
Basement — 1,221 sq. ft.
Garage — 436 sq. ft.

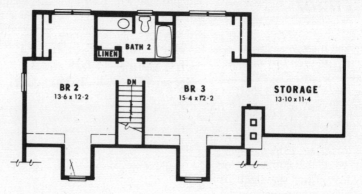

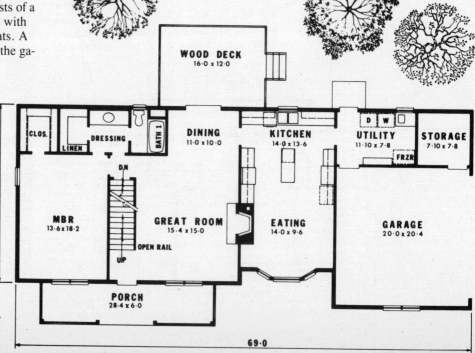

Luxurious Master Suite

No. 90329

On the second floor, the roomy master bedroom with its luxurious master bath and dressing area will be a constant delight. Just a step down from the bedroom itself, the bath incorporates an oversized corner tub, a shower, a walk-in closet, and a skylight. The third bedroom could serve as a loft or sitting room. The open staircase spirals down to the first floor great room with its vaulted ceiling, fireplace, and corner of windows. The adjacent dining room has a wet bar and direct access to the large, eat-in kitchen. Additional living space is provided by the family room which opens onto the deck through sliding glass doors.

Main floor — 904 sq. ft.
Upper floor — 797 sq. ft.
Basement — 904 sq. ft.
Garage — 405 sq. ft.

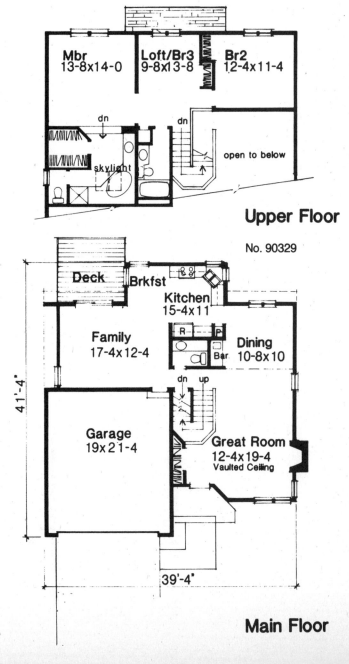

Upper Floor

No. 90329

Main Floor

Arches Grace Classic Facade

No. 10677

Do you have a small lot, but love open space? Here's your answer! This compact beauty uses built-in planters and half-walls to define rooms without closing them in. Look at the first floor plan. The living room features a cozy sitting area dominated by a half-round window, then rises to nearly two stories for a wide-open feeling. At the rear of the house, the family room and kitchen, divided only by a cooktop peninsula, share the airy atmosphere. Sliders unite this sunny area with an outdoor patio that mirrors the shape of the dining bay. Peer down at the living room from your vantage point on the balcony that connects the three bedrooms upstairs. And, be sure to notice the double sinks and built-in vanity in the master bath, a plus when you're rushed in the morning.

First floor — 932 sq. ft.
Second floor — 764 sq. ft.
Garage — 430 sq. ft.
Basement — 920 sq. ft.

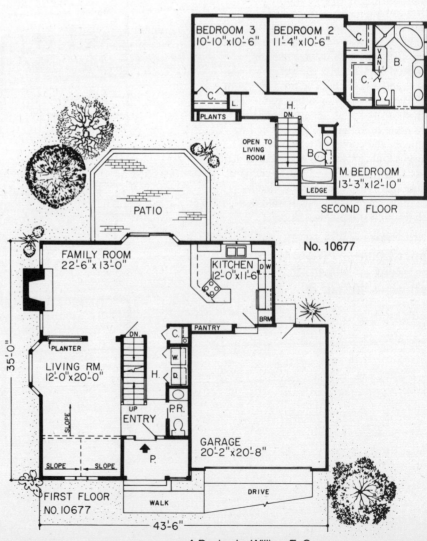

A Design by William E. Gage

Abundant Windows Add Outdoor Feeling

No. 99310

Now, here's a three-bedroom house your family will want to call home. From its traditional front porch to the breakfast bay overlooking the patio, this country charmer has an inviting appeal that's hard to resist. And, with conveniences like a built-in bar in the dining room, an efficient kitchen with a range-top island, built-in planning desk and pantry, and two-and-a-half baths to accommodate your busy family, you won't want to resist! Add the excitement of a vaulted, fireplaced living room with windows on three sides, an open staircase flooded with natural light, and a dramatic master suite with private, double-vanitied bath, and you've got the perfect place to raise your family.

First floor — 1,160 sq. ft.
Second floor — 797 sq. ft.
Garage — 2-car

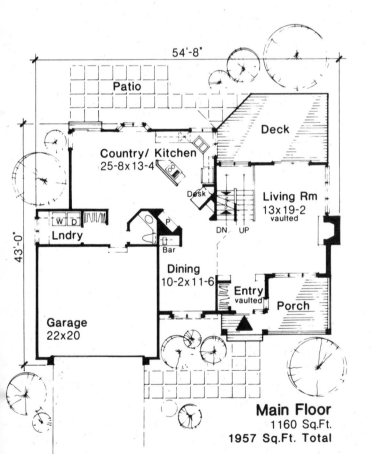

Main Floor
1160 Sq.Ft.
1957 Sq.Ft. Total

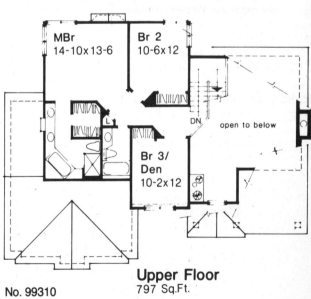

No. 99310

Upper Floor
797 Sq.Ft.

Corner Entry Adds Delightful Angles

No. 99302

Watch the world go by from your breakfast room vantage point in this exquisite, one-level classic designed for easy living. A distinctive corner entry adds an angular quality to the exciting, vaulted spaces of the living and dining rooms. With abundant windows and a wraparound rear deck, this area boasts a wonderful, outdoor feeling. And, when you're entertaining, the open kitchen-breakfast room combination has ample space for an army of cooks, along with pass-over convenience to the dining room. Three bedrooms and two full baths, including the vaulted master suite at the rear of the house, complete this compact plan.

Main living area — 1,270 sq. ft.
Garage — 2-car

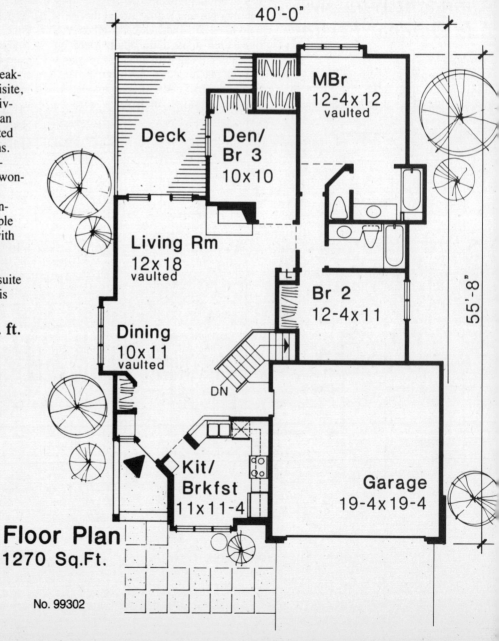

40'-0"

55'-8"

Deck

Den/ Br 3
10x10

MBr
12-4x12
vaulted

Living Rm
12x18
vaulted

Br 2
12-4x11

Dining
10x11
vaulted

DN

Kit/ Brkfst
11x11-4

Garage
19-4x19-4

Floor Plan
1270 Sq.Ft.

No. 99302

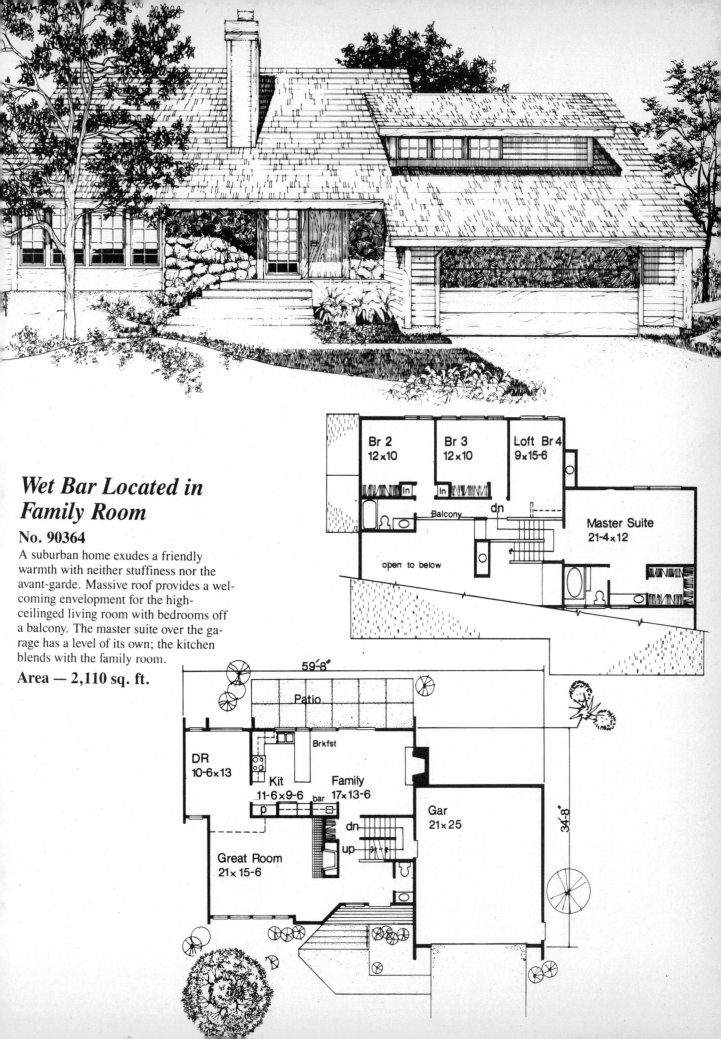

Wet Bar Located in Family Room

No. 90364

A suburban home exudes a friendly warmth with neither stuffiness nor the avant-garde. Massive roof provides a welcoming envelopment for the high-ceilinged living room with bedrooms off a balcony. The master suite over the garage has a level of its own; the kitchen blends with the family room.

Area — 2,110 sq. ft.

Br 2
12 x10

Br 3
12 x10

Loft Br 4
9 x15-6

Balcony

dn

Master Suite
21-4 x12

open to below

59'-8"

Patio

Brkfst

DR
10-6 x13

Kit
11-6 x9-6

Family
17 x13-6

bar

Gar
21 x 25

34-8"

dn

p

up

Great Room
21 x 15-6

Striking Entryway

No. 20054

An expansive entrance with a cathedral ceiling in the living room offers a view of the entire house. The washer and dryer are located in the bedroom area, and even with small square footage, this home has a large master bedroom area and separate dining room and breakfast area. The deck is partially under the roof. The roof framing on this plan is simple, but the exterior is still interesting due to the large windows and the farmhouse porch.

First floor — 1,461 sq. ft.
Basement — 1,435 sq. ft.
Garage — 528 sq. ft.

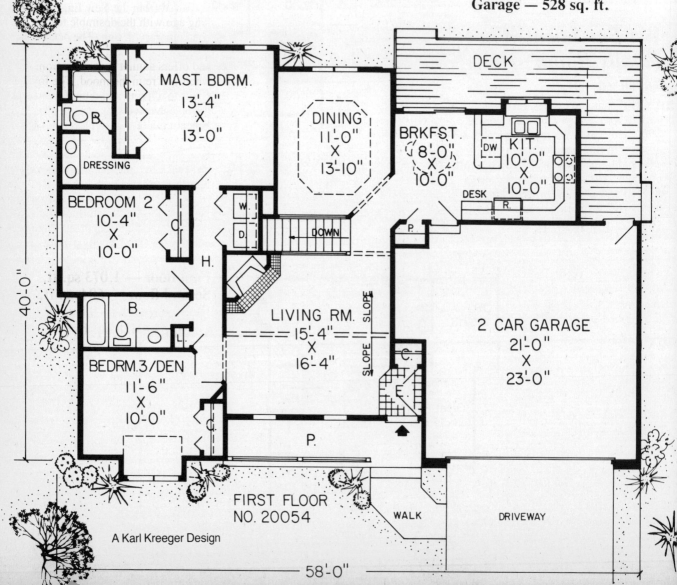

FIRST FLOOR
NO. 20054

A Karl Kreeger Design

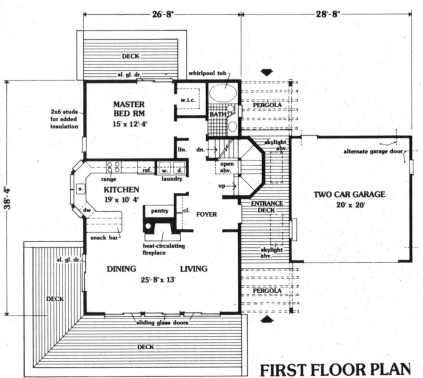

26'-8" **28'-8"**

DECK

sl. gl. dr. whirlpool tub

w.i.c.

MASTER
BED RM
15' x 12'-4"

BATH

2x6 studs
for added
insulation

PERGOLA

skylight abv.

lin. dn.

ref. w. d.

range laundry

KITCHEN
19' x 10' 4"

open
abv.

s.

dw

up

pantry cl.

snack bar

heat-circulating
fireplace

ENTRANCE
DECK

alternate garage door

TWO CAR GARAGE
20' x 20'

FOYER

38'-4"

DINING LIVING
25'-8" x 13'

sl. gl. dr.

skylight
abv.

DECK

PERGOLA

sliding glass doors

DECK

No. 90685

FIRST FLOOR PLAN

skylight above

roof

BED RM
13'-8" x 12'-4"

cl.

BATH

dn.

TOWER
RETREAT

dn.

open

BED RM
16' x 11'-4"

cl.

up to
tower

lin. BALC.

railing

high ceiling

dining / living below

roof

high windows

SECOND FLOOR PLAN

Farmhouse Flavor

No. 90685

This exciting home combines elements
borrowed from the New England barns of
long ago with the desirable features of
contemporary design. The octagonal stair
tower is sure to be a conversation piece,
and offers a quiet spot away from it all
when you're in the mood. The foyer
opens to a living and dining room combination enhanced by a striking glass wall.
A heat-circulating fireplace adds welcome warmth when the sun goes down.
The galley kitchen includes a large pantry, snack bar, and laundry area. The
first-floor master suite has a private deck
overlooking the backyard, as well as a
luxurious bath with whirlpool tub. Two
bedrooms and a full bath share the second floor with a balcony overlooking the
living room.

First floor — 1,073 sq. ft.
Second floor — 604 sq. ft.
Retreat tower — 93 sq. ft.
Garage — 428 sq. ft.

Contemporary and Convenient

No. 90542

Arches add graceful appeal both inside and outside this exciting, three-bedroom contemporary. An angular, two-story entry dominated by an elegant staircase provides easy access to every room on the main floor, from the soaring spaces of the fireplaced living room to the well-appointed kitchen. The bay-windowed nook just over the counter is cheerful and bright. Dining and family rooms at the rear of the house share access to the rear patio, along with a back yard view in two directions. A handy chute at the top of the stairs makes your job easier on laundry day. Two skylit baths serve the bedrooms, which include a luxurious master suite with a private living room vantage point.

First floor — 980 sq. ft.
Second floor — 855 sq. ft.
Loft — 100 sq. ft.
Garage — 2-car

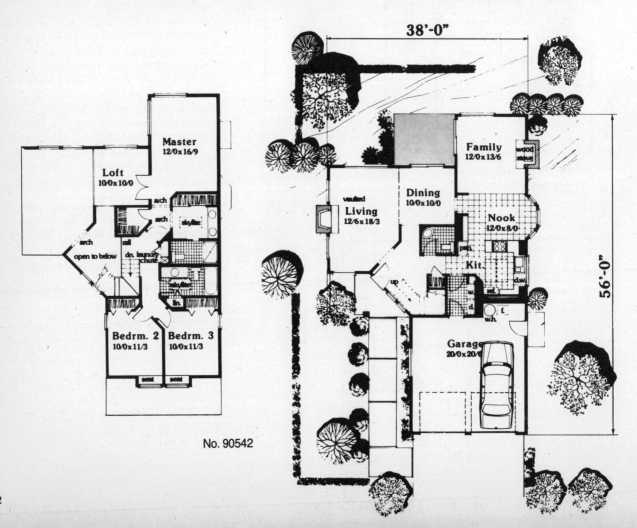

No. 90542

Lots of Space in this Small Package

No. 90378

Here's a compact gem that won't break your budget. Well-placed windows, an open plan, and vaulted ceilings lend a spacious feeling to this contemporary home. The dynamic, soaring angles of the living room are accentuated by the fireplace that dominates the room. Eat in the dining room adjoining the kitchen, or step through the sliders for dinner on the deck. And, when it's time to make coffee in the morning, you'll love the first-floor location of the master suite, just steps away from the kitchen. Upstairs, a full bath serves two bedrooms, each with a walk-in closet.

First floor — 878 sq. ft.
Second floor — 405 sq. ft.
Garage — 2-car

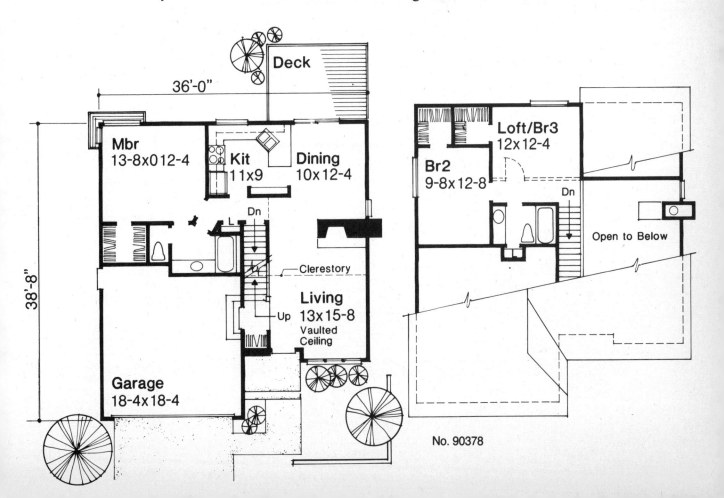

No. 90378

FRONT ELEVATION

FLOOR PLAN

67' 2"

50' 0"

SUN ROOM

PATIO

BREAKFAST
9'-10" x 10'-0"

KITCHEN

MASTER BEDROOM
20'-4" x 15'-6"

DRESS

LIVING ROOM
18'-6" x 17'-6"

DINING
10'-6" x 11'-0"

BATH

FOYER

BEDROOM
13'-6" x 12'-0"

BEDROOM
13'-6" x 11'-8"

GARAGE
21'-0" x 21'-0"

Passive Solar With Sun Room

No. 90417

This ranch design features large areas of glass in the master suite and kitchen, and a sun room accessible from both the family room and breakfast room. A recessed entry and a limited amount of glass on the north wall help keep the warm air in during the winter, and over-heating during the summer months is prevented by eliminating glass from the east and west walls. The master suite features a walk-in closet and a compartmentalized bath with linen closet, a second walk-in closet and a dressing area with double vanity. One of the two front bedrooms has a double closet and direct access to a second full bath and the other has a walk-in-closet. A centrally located utility closet and two hall closets complete the left wing. Separating the sunken living room and the foyer area is a massive stone fireplace. A formal dining room can be entered from either the living room or the kitchen. The U-shaped kitchen has a bar counter open to the breakfast area and a mud room with coat closet and access to the garage which acts as a buffer from northwestern winter winds.

Area — 1,859 sq. ft.

SOUTH ELEVATION

Another Nice Ranch Design

No. 90354

Small and move-up houses are looking much larger these days thanks to clever proportions and roof masses, as exemplified in this two-bedroom ranch. The inside space seems larger, from the high-impact entrance with through-views to the vaulted great room, fireplace, and rear deck. The den (optional third bedroom) features double doors. The kitchen & breakfast area has a vaulted ceiling. The plan easily adapts to crawl or slab construction with utilities replacing stairs, laundry facing the kitchen, and air handler and water heater facing the garage.

Living Area — 1,360 sq. ft.

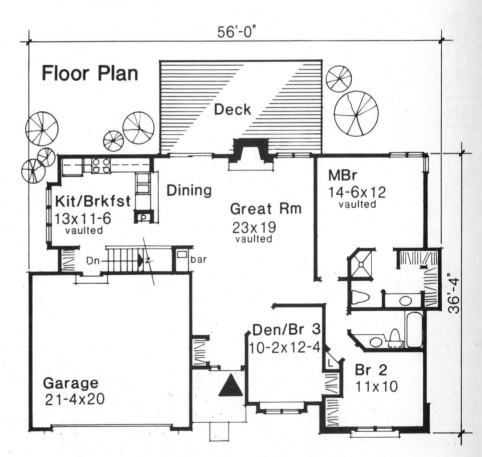

Floor Plan

56'-0"

Deck

Dining

Kit/Brkfst
13x11-6
vaulted

Great Rm
23x19
vaulted

MBr
14-6x12
vaulted

Dn   bar

Garage
21-4x20

Den/Br 3
10-2x12-4

Br 2
11x10

36'-4"

No. 90354

Three Private Dressing Rooms

No. 90039

The front and rear exposed living room with its log burning fireplace and covered rear porch, the double access family room, the curved walled dining room with porch entry, and kitchen providing a circular breakfast nook, planning desk and concealed laundry make up the impressive balance of the first floor. The second floor, comfortably housing three large bedrooms offers unique features: a balconied hall, three private dressing rooms, large four-fixture bath with two windows, luxurious closet space and a master bedroom suite with private bath, three rear sky windows, four front windows and a 15 x 20 foot storage room.

First floor — 1,064 sq. ft.
Second floor — 947 sq. ft.

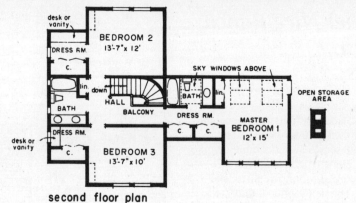

second floor plan

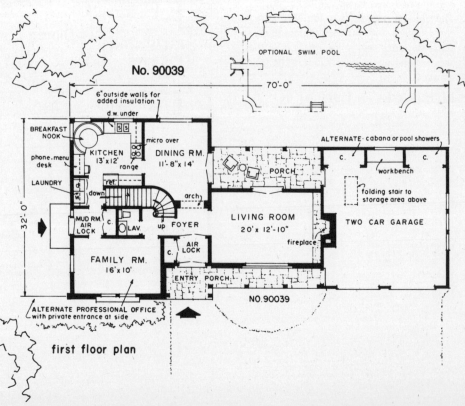

first floor plan

Traditional Character for Today's Family

No. 90213

Here's a classic plan designed for a growing family. A covered porch offers shelter for the central entry that leads two ways: into the sunny, formal living room, and back to family areas at the rear of the house. Sliding glass doors unite both the formal dining and fireplaced family rooms with the rear terrace for an out-door feeling. Whether you're dining in formal style or snacking in the sunken family room, you'll love the convenience of the centrally located kitchen. You'll also enjoy the master suite overlooking the backyard, which includes a private bath with step-in shower. Three more second-floor bedrooms share a handy hall bath.

First floor — 1,042 sq. ft.
Second floor — 780 sq. ft.
Garage — 2-car

WALK-IN CLOSET

SLOPED CEILING

BATH

LINEN

STORAGE

HALL

BEDROOM
13'-6" X 13'-4"

RAIL

OPEN

DOWN

LINEN

WALK-IN CLOSET

BEDROOM
12'-4" X 15'-4"

SECOND FLOOR

Basement with Drive-Under Garage

No. 90401

This rustic design includes a two-car garage as part of its full basement. All or part of the basement can be used to supplement the main living area. The master suite features a large walk-in closet and a double vanity in the master bath. An L-shaped kitchen with dining bay, a living room with raised-hearth fireplace and a centrally located utility room complete the main floor. The open two-story foyer leads to the upper floor consisting of two bedrooms with walk-in closets and a second full bath with two linen closets. Front porch, multi-paned windows, shutters and horizontal wood siding combine for a rustic exterior. Basement foundation only.

First floor — 1,100 sq. ft.
Second floor — 660 sq. ft.

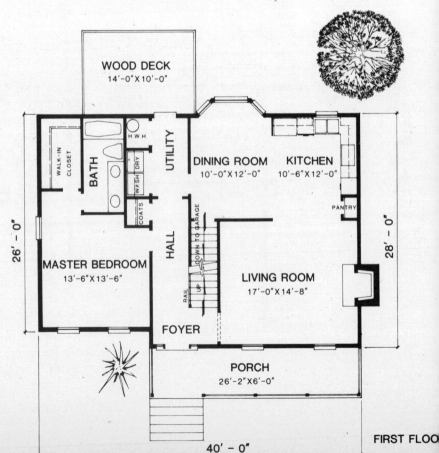

WOOD DECK
14'-0" X 10'-0"

WALK-IN CLOSET

BATH

H W H

WASH DRY

COATS

UTILITY

DINING ROOM
10'-0" X 12'-0"

KITCHEN
10'-6" X 12'-0"

PANTRY

26'-0"

MASTER BEDROOM
13'-6" X 13'-6"

HALL

DOWN TO GARAGE

RAIL

UP

LIVING ROOM
17'-0" X 14'-8"

28'-0"

FOYER

PORCH
26'-2" X 6'-0"

40'-0"

FIRST FLOO

Open Living Area Plus Traditional Styling

No. 90107

The great room concept in this traditional home combines the kitchen, dining and living areas into one integrated space. Each of the two large bedrooms has its own complete bath. The master bedroom incorporates a spacious walk-in closet. Perfect for adult living and entertaining, this home also features a two car garage with plenty of storage or space for a workshop.

Living Area — 1,092 sq. ft.

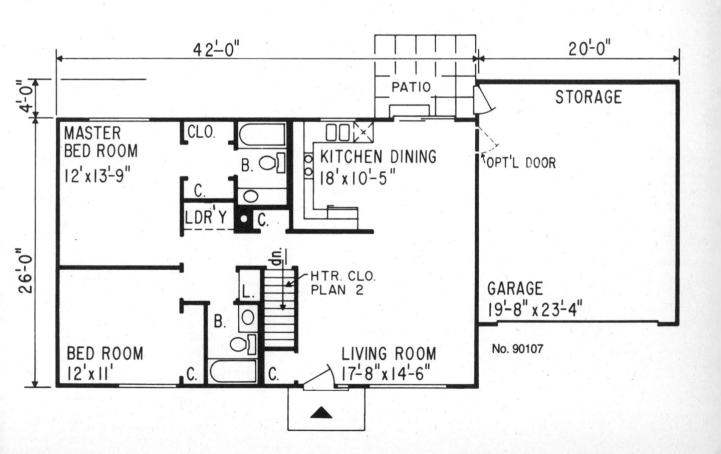

MASTER BED ROOM 12'x13'-9"

CLO.

B.

C.

LDR'Y   C.

KITCHEN DINING 18'x10'-5"

PATIO

STORAGE

OPT'L DOOR

42'-0"   20'-0"

4'-0"

26'-0"

BED ROOM 12'x11"

B.

C.   C.

dn.

L.

HTR. CLO. PLAN 2

GARAGE 19'-8" x 23'-4"

LIVING ROOM 17'-8"x14'-6"

No. 90107

Use the Deck off the Master Suite for Private Sunbaths

No. 91411

Orient this charming sun-catcher to the south, add the optional sunspace off the dining room, and you'll have a solar home without equal. The sunken living room, formal dining room, and island kitchen with adjoining, informal nook all enjoy an expansive view of the patio and back yard beyond. A fireplace in the living room, and a wood stove separating the nook and family room keep the house toasty when the sun goes down. The sunny atmosphere found on the first floor continues upstairs, where skylights brighten the balcony and master bath.

And, with three bedrooms on the upper floor, and one downstairs, you can promise the kids their own rooms. Specify crawlspace or basement when ordering this plan.

First floor — 1,249 sq. ft.
Second floor — 890 sq. ft.
Garage — 462 sq. ft.

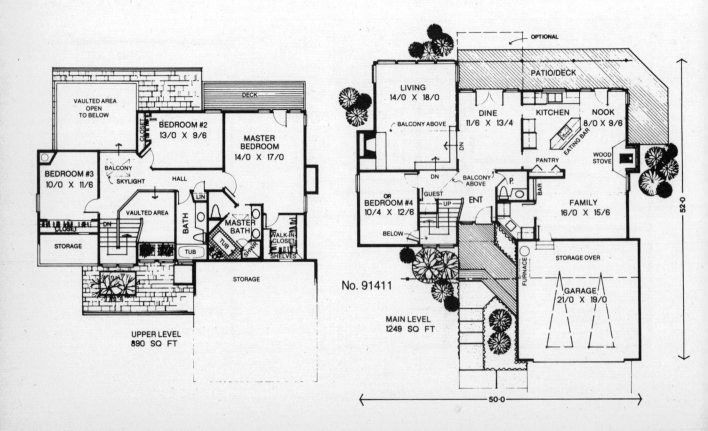

Old American Saltbox Design

No. 90123

A sloping ceiling creates a sense of spaciousness for this modest design. Relax in front of the centrally located fireplace in cool weather or move through triple sliding glass doors to the roomy deck when weather is warmer. Behind the living room lies a bedroom, full bath and kitchen/dining area which has a window seat. Laundry facilities are conveniently placed off the kitchen. On the left of the living room a quiet corner has been tucked under the stairs leading to the second floor. The second level affords two nice sized bedrooms (one with its own private deck), joined by a full bath. A balcony skirts the entire level and overlooks the living room below.

First floor — 840 sq. ft.
Second floor — 440 sq. ft.

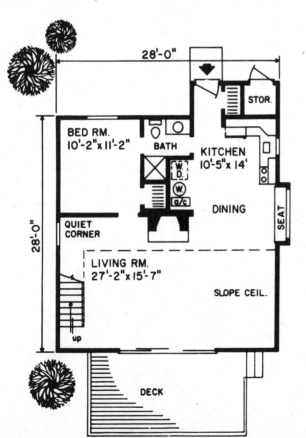

FIRST FLOOR

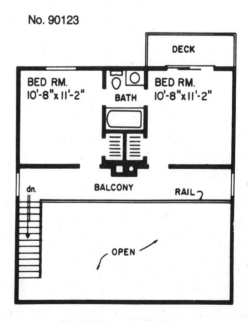

SECOND FLOOR

Screened Porch Designed For Dining

No. 8262

This three bedroom, two bath design has a screened porch adjacent to the dining room which offers sheltered open air dining. A corner fireplace in the living room and the unique expanse of windows create a certain ambiance repeated in the airy, yet efficient kitchen. The master bedroom merits a full bath.

First floor — 1,406 sq. ft.
Basement — 1,394 sq. ft.
Garage — 444 sq. ft.

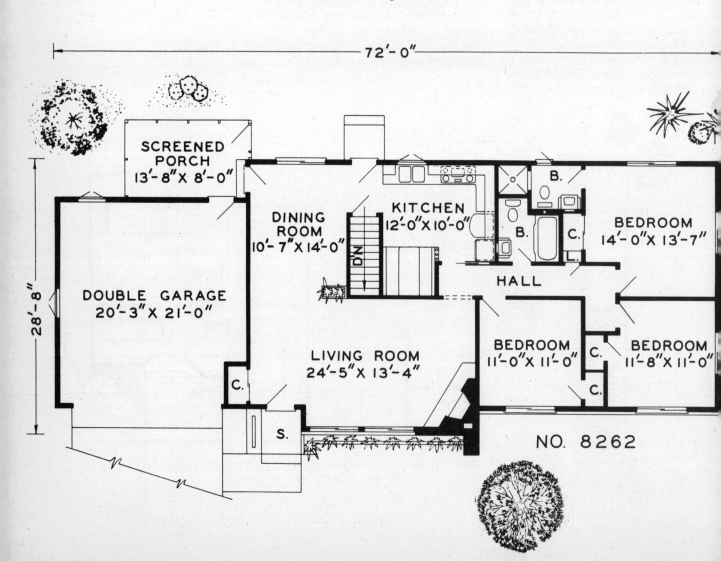

72'-0"

28'-8"

SCREENED PORCH
13'-8" X 8'-0"

DINING ROOM
10'-7" X 14'-0"

KITCHEN
12'-0" X 10'-0"

DOUBLE GARAGE
20'-3" X 21'-0"

D'N

B.

B.

B.

C.

BEDROOM
14'-0" X 13'-7"

HALL

C.

LIVING ROOM
24'-5" X 13'-4"

BEDROOM
11'-0" X 11'-0"

C.

C.

BEDROOM
11'-8" X 11'-0"

C.

S.

NO. 8262

Contemporary Classic with a Custom Look

No. 99314

A curving staircase lit from above crowns the entry of this beautiful wood and fieldstone contemporary. To the right, a well-apppointed kitchen features an angular nook just perfect for your breakfast table. The great room straight ahead soars two stories, for an outdoor feeling accentuated by a massive fireplace and sliders to the rear deck. Corner windows make the dining area a pleasant spot to enjoy a dinner with friends. To the left, past the powder room, the master suite features a bump-out window seat, and a private bath with double vanities. An open loft overlooking the great room shares the second floor with a second bedroom and another full bath.

First floor — 1,044 sq. ft.
Second floor — 454 sq. ft.
Garage — 2-car

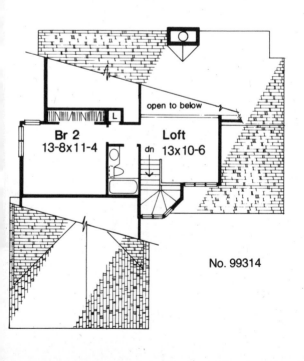

No. 99314

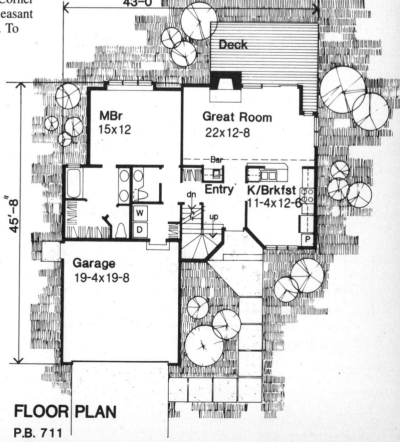

FLOOR PLAN
P.B. 711
1498 Sq. Ft.

Rustic Warmth

No. 90440

While the covered porch and huge, field-stone fireplace lend a rustic air to this three-bedroom classic, the interior is loaded with the amenities you've been seeking. Doesn't a book-lined, fireplaced living room sound nice? Haven't you been longing for a fully-equipped island kitchen? This one adjoins a sunny dining room with sliders to a wood deck. Does the idea of a first-floor master suite just steps away from your morning coffee sound good? Tucked upstairs with another full bath, two bedrooms feature walk-in closets and cozy, sloping ceilings. There's even plenty of extra storage space in the attic.

First floor — 1,100 sq. ft.
Second floor — 664 sq. ft.
Basement — 1,100 sq. ft.

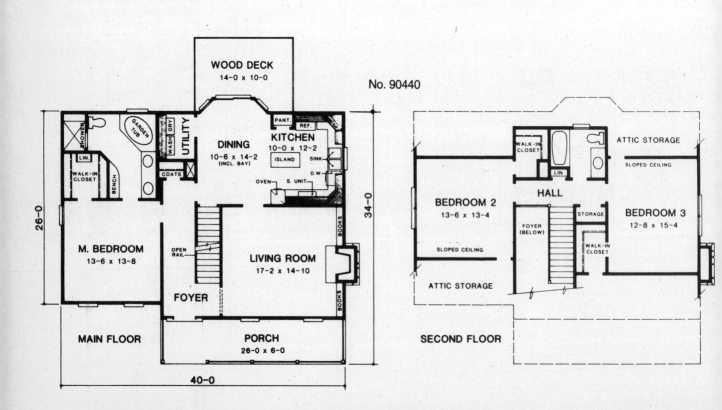

No. 90440

WOOD DECK
14-0 x 10-0

GARDEN TUB

SHOWER

LIN.

WALK-IN CLOSET

BENCH

WASH DRY

UTILITY

COATS

PANT.

DINING
10-6 x 14-2
(INCL. BAY)

KITCHEN
10-0 x 12-2

REF.

ISLAND

SINK

D.W.

OVEN

S. UNIT

26-0

M. BEDROOM
13-6 x 13-8

OPEN RAIL

LIVING ROOM
17-2 x 14-10

BOOKS

34-0

FOYER

BOOKS

MAIN FLOOR

PORCH
26-0 x 6-0

40-0

WALK-IN CLOSET

LIN.

ATTIC STORAGE

SLOPED CEILING

BEDROOM 2
13-6 x 13-4

HALL

STORAGE

BEDROOM 3
12-8 x 15-4

FOYER (BELOW)

SLOPED CEILING

WALK-IN CLOSET

ATTIC STORAGE

SECOND FLOOR

Rural Farmhouse Profile

No. 26001

A varied gabled roof, a large railed front porch and wood create a picturesque rural farmhouse profile in this plan. On the lower level a central hallway channels traffic easily to all rooms — a spacious formal living room and family-dining area with a bay window and fireplace in the front, and a bedroom suite, utility area, and kitchen at the back. A mud room is suitably located adjacent to the utility area. A sheltered outside entrance to the utility room and the double garage is given by a breezeway-porch. On the second level three bedrooms nearly encircle a center bath.

First floor — 1,184 sq. ft.
Second floor — 821 sq. ft.
Basement — 821 sq. ft.
Garage — 576 sq. ft.
Front porch — 176 sq. ft.
Side porch — 69 sq. ft.

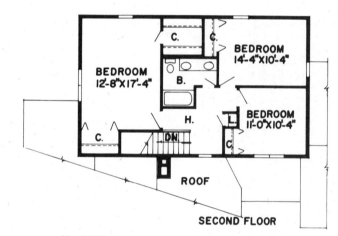

SECOND FLOOR

No. 26001

FIRST FLOOR

NO. 26001

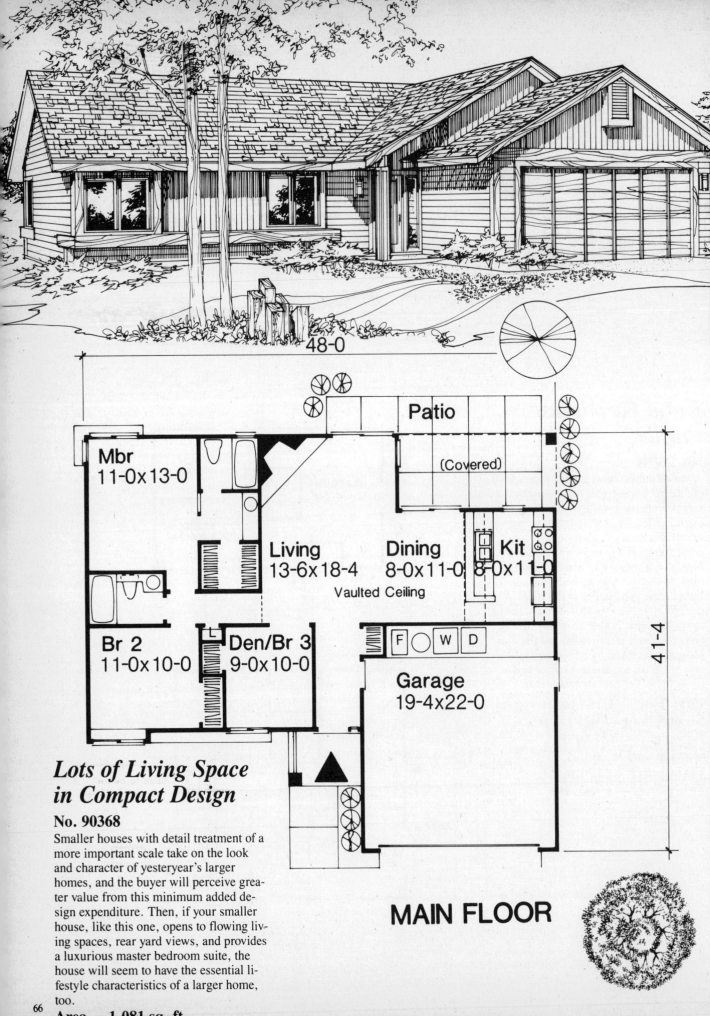

Patio

(Covered)

Mbr
11-0 x 13-0

Living
13-6 x 18-4

Dining
8-0 x 11-0

Kit
8-0 x 11-0

Vaulted Ceiling

Br 2
11-0 x 10-0

Den/Br 3
9-0 x 10-0

F W D

Garage
19-4 x 22-0

48-0

41-4

Lots of Living Space in Compact Design

No. 90368

Smaller houses with detail treatment of a more important scale take on the look and character of yesteryear's larger homes, and the buyer will perceive greater value from this minimum added design expenditure. Then, if your smaller house, like this one, opens to flowing living spaces, rear yard views, and provides a luxurious master bedroom suite, the house will seem to have the essential lifestyle characteristics of a larger home, too.

Area — 1,081 sq. ft.

MAIN FLOOR

Lattice Trim Adds Nostalgic Charm

No. 99315

Thanks to vaulted ceilings and an ingenious plan, this wood and fieldstone classic feels much larger than its compact size. The entry, dominated by a skylit staircase to the bedroom floor, opens to the vaulted living room with a balcony view and floor-to-ceiling corner window treatment. Eat in the spacious, formal dining room, in the sunny breakfast nook off the kitchen, or, when the weather's nice, out on the adjoining deck. Pass-through convenience makes meal service easy wherever you choose to dine. A full bath at the top of the stairs serves the kids' bedrooms off the balcony hall. But, the master suite boasts its own, private bath, along with a private dressing area.

First floor — 668 sq. ft.
Second floor — 691 sq. ft.
Garage — 2-car

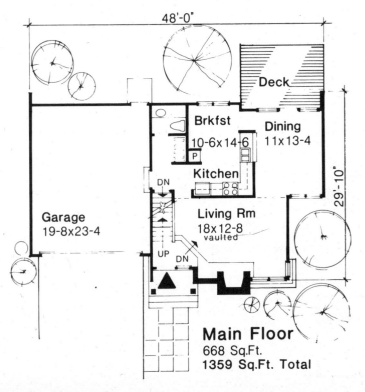

Main Floor
668 Sq.Ft.
1359 Sq.Ft. Total

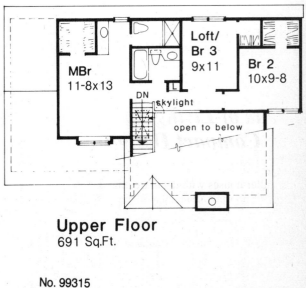

Upper Floor
691 Sq.Ft.

No. 99315

Three Bedroom Features Cathedral Ceilings

No. 20051

The tiled foyer of this charming house rises to the second floor balcony and is lighted by a circular window. To the right of the foyer are the powder room, the compact laundry area, and the entrance to the well-designed kitchen. The kitchen features a central island, built-in desk, pantry, and adjacent breakfast area. The combined living and dining room enjoys a fireplace, built-in bookcase, and sloped ceiling.

First floor — 1,285 sq. ft.
Second floor — 490 sq. ft.
Basement — 1,285 sq.f t.
Garage — 495 sq. ft.

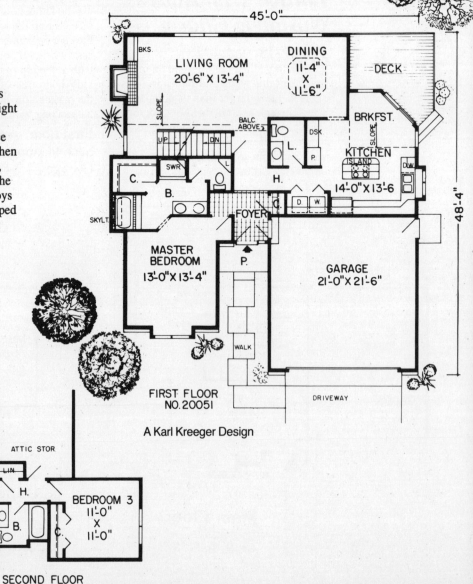

FIRST FLOOR
NO. 20051

A Karl Kreeger Design

SECOND FLOOR

Den Offers Peaceful Haven

No. 90923

Here is an exquisite victorian adaptation. The exterior, with its interesting roof lines, window treatment, and inviting entrance porch, could hardly be more dramatic. Inside, the delightfully large, two-story foyer has a beautiful curved staircase and controls the flexible traffic patterns. There's loads of room in this house for formal entertaining. For the family's informal acitvities, family room, covered patio, nook and kitchen areas conveniently interact. Notice the large pantry in the kitchen. Upstairs, via an open balcony hall, you'll find four spacious bedrooms, including the lovely master suite with lavish, sunken tub.

Main floor — 1,264 sq. ft.
Second floor — 1,001 sq. ft.
Basement — 1,264 sq. ft.
Garage — 441 sq. ft.
Width — 42 ft.
Depth — 56 ft.

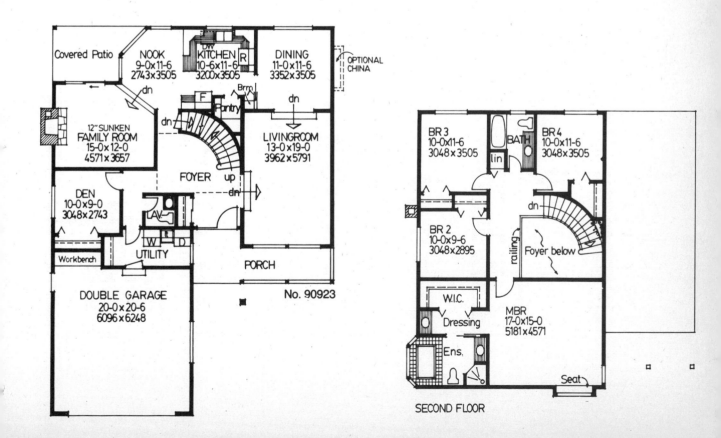

Expansive, Not Expensive

No. 90623

Despite its compact area, this home looks and lives like a luxurious ranch. A decorative screen divides the entrance foyer from the spacious, comfortable living room, which flows into the pleasant dining room overlooking a rear garden. The roomy, eat-in kitchen features a planning corner. And, the adjacent laundry-mud-room provides access to the two-car garage and to the outdoors. Here also lie the stairs to the full basement, a valuable, functional part of the house which adds many possibilities for informal family living. The private bedroom wing includes three bedrooms and two baths.

Total living area — 1,370 sq. ft.

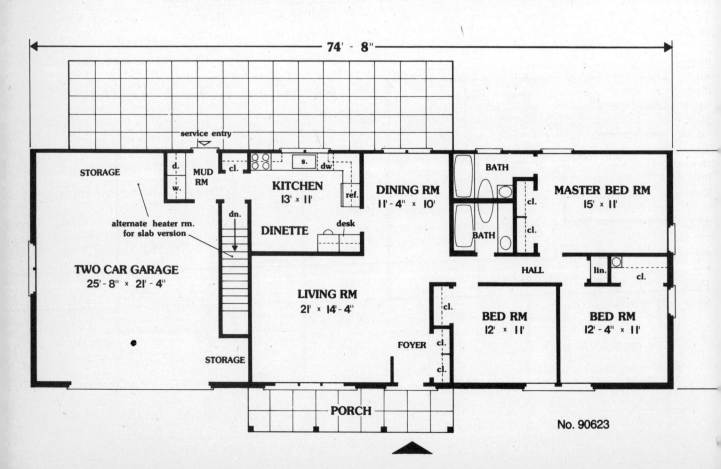

Appealing Home Deserves Beautiful Setting

No. 90208

This compact family home combines rustic and modern elements for a wide-open plan with wide-ranging appeal. The entry hall opens to the towering gathering room with a two-story view. Step back to the kitchen and dining room, which enjoy the toasty atmosphere of the fireplace oven, and the warm-weather convenience of an outdoor dining deck. Tucked behind the sun-washed, U-shaped staircase, the first-floor master suite is brightened by a bump-out window, and features a private bath with dressing room and double vanities. Watch the action below from the lounge overlooking the gathering room, which shares the second floor with two spacious bedrooms and a full bath.

First floor — 1,113 sq. ft.
Second floor — 543 sq. ft.

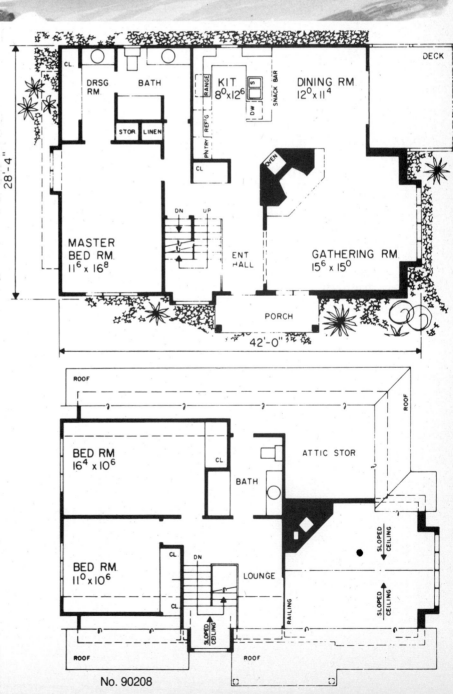

No. 90208

Graceful Elegance, Family-Style

No. 91020

A towering bay gives this beautiful home an impressive facade. Inside, the drama continues. Vaulted ceilings add a spacious airiness to the central entry, living, dining, and master bedrooms. You'll find a cheerful atmosphere throughout the house. Abundant windows and an open plan give the bayed family room, nook and kitchen a sunny warmth. Upstairs, the four bedrooms and two full baths include the luxurious master suite, dominated by a huge, half-round bay window.

Total living area — 2,157 sq. ft.

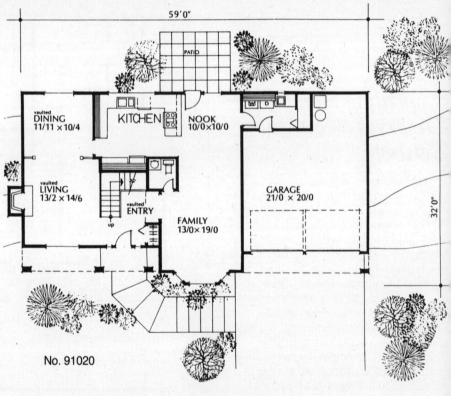

No. 91020

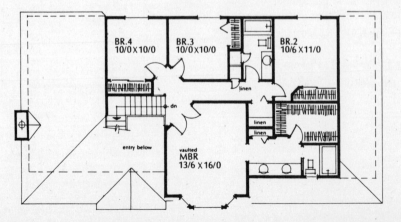

Passive Solar and Contemporary Features

No. 26110

Numerous south facing glass doors and windows, skylights and a greenhouse clue the exterior viewer to this passive solar contemporary design. For minimum heat loss, 2x6 studs for R-19 insulation are used in exterior walls, and R-33 insulation is used in all sloping ceilings. The living room employs a concrete slab floor for solar gain. Basement space is located under the kitchen, dining room, lower bedroom and den. A northern entrance through a vestibule and French doors channels you upward to the first floor living area. A unique feature on this level is the skylit living room ceiling which slants two stories. Second story rooms are lit by clerestory windows. Two balconies are on this level: an exterior one off the bedroom and an interior one overlooking the living room.

First floor — 902 sq. ft.
Second floor — 567 sq. ft.

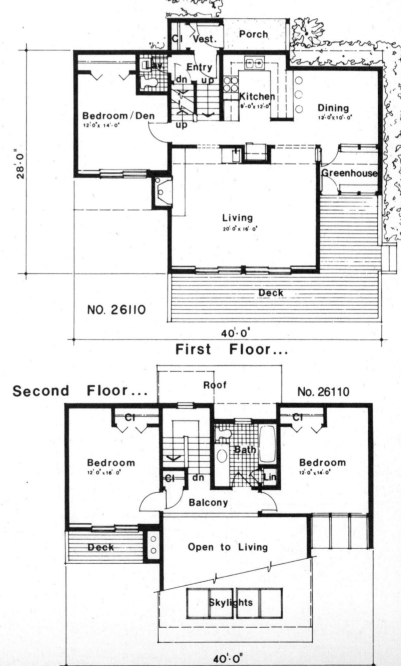

Room for Family Activities

No. 10649

With two covered porches and a brick patio, this traditional Cape is an inviting abode for your outdoor-loving family. The central entry leads down a hallway to the family room. Warmed by a fireplace and boasting a wet bar, lots of windows and french doors, this enormous room is a great gathering place. Serve meals in the bay-windowed breakfast nook or the formal dining room located on either side of the kitchen. Window seats adorning the front bedrooms upstairs provide a pleasant retreat for quiet moments.

First floor — 1,285 sq. ft.
Second floor — 930 sq. ft.
Garage — 492 sq. ft.

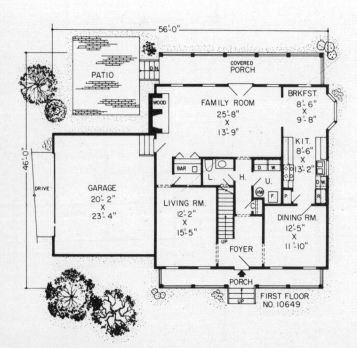

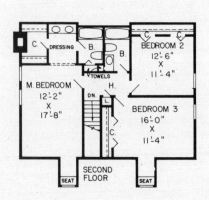

Multi-level Contemporary

No. 26111

The features of this multi-level contemporary home lend character to both the exterior and interior. A wooden deck skirts most of three sides. The variety in the size and shape of doors and windows adds charm. Inside, the living room forms a unique living center. It can be reached from sliding glass doors from the deck or down several steps from the main living level inside. It is overlooked by a low balcony from the entryway and dining room on the lower level and from the second floor landing. Large windows on both the right and the left keep it well lit. A fireplace here is optional. Ceilings slope upward two stories. A partial basement is located below the design.

First floor — 769 sq. ft.
Second floor — 572 sq. ft.

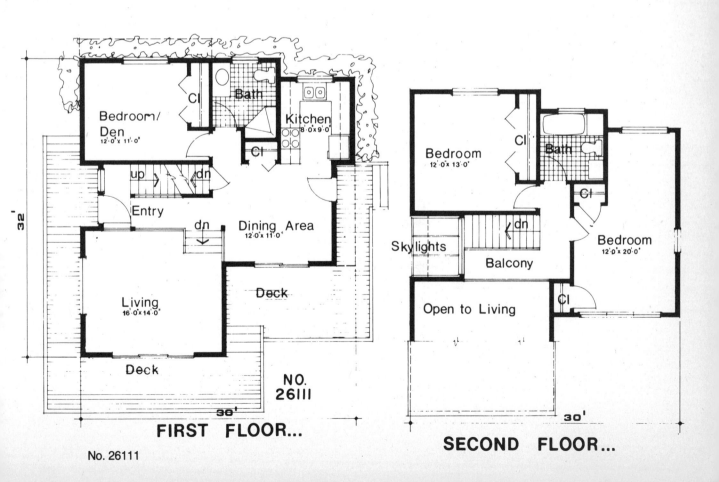

FIRST FLOOR...

No. 26111

SECOND FLOOR...

Inexpensive Ranch Design

No. 20062

This attractive, inexpensive ranch home has a brick and vertical siding exterior. The interior has a well set-up kitchen area with its own breakfast area by a large picture window. A formal dining room is located near the kitchen. The living room has one open beam across a sloping ceiling. A large hearth is in front of a woodburning fireplace. Inside the front entrance a tiled foyer incorporates closet space and has many different room entrances through which an individual can walk. The master bedroom has an extremely large bath area with its own walk-in closet. Two other bedrooms share a full bath. There is also a linen closet and a closet for the washer and dryer area. A two-car garage is offered in this plan.

First floor — 1,500 sq. ft.
Basement — 1,500 sq. ft.
Garage — 482 sq. ft.

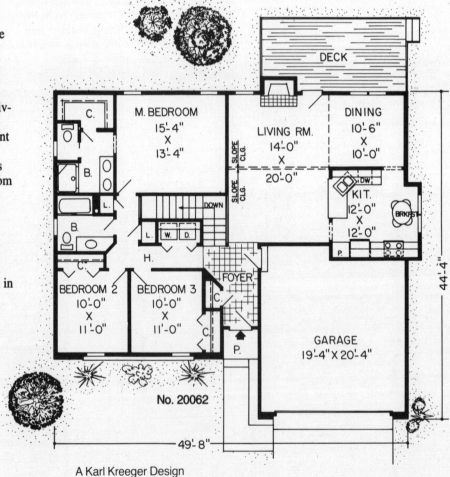

No. 20062

A Karl Kreeger Design

Bright and Beautiful

No. 91008

Imagine the attention the brightly-lit stair tower of this smart contemporary will attract after dark. From the bay-windowed kitchen and bedroom to the fire-placed living room, the angles of the tower are mirrored in the shapes of every room. Watch your guests arrive from the convenient kitchen at the front of the house or the balcony upstairs. You'll enjoy the privacy of entertaining in the formal dining room at the rear of the house, or the covered patio just outside. At day's end, the master suite is a roomy and welcoming retreat.

First floor — 1,153 sq. ft.
Second floor — 493 sq. ft.

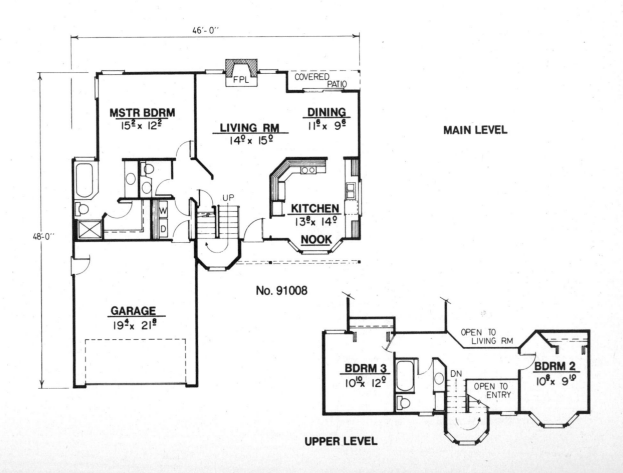

46'- 0"

48'- 0"

FPL

COVERED PATIO

MSTR BDRM
15² x 12²

LIVING RM
14⁰ x 15⁰

DINING
11⁸ x 9⁸

MAIN LEVEL

UP

W
D

KITCHEN
13⁸ x 14⁰

NOOK

GARAGE
19⁴ x 21⁸

No. 91008

OPEN TO LIVING RM

BDRM 3
10¹⁰ x 12⁰

DN

OPEN TO ENTRY

BDRM 2
10⁸ x 9¹⁰

UPPER LEVEL

Modest Tudor With A Massive Look

No. 90012

Specifically designed to make its presence felt in any neighborhood, this stately Tudor home contains fewer square feet, and is more affordable, than one would imagine. Broken and steeply sloping roof lines, dormers, a large cantilevered bay, and a Gothic shaped, unique entrance way —as well as the charming stone, brick, and half-timber materials— all add keen interest to the exterior. The living/dining space is an open 34 ft. area designed to be an impressive focal point; a large log burning fireplace is centrally located on the far wall. The triple windows in the front allow for a grand view.

**First floor — 1,078 sq. ft.
Second floor — 1,131 sq. ft.**

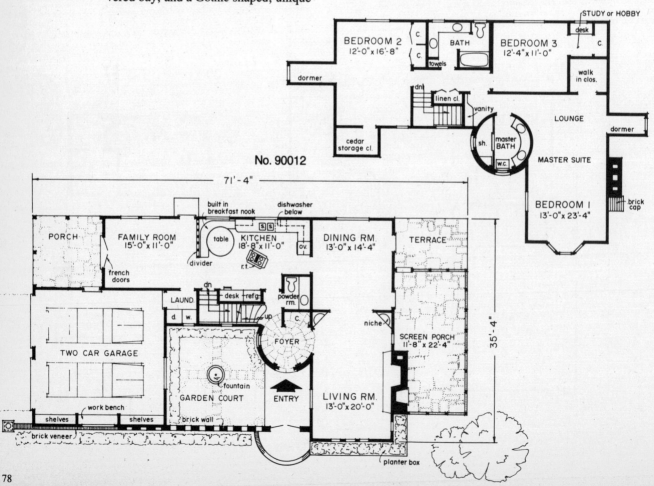

Multi-Level Home Boasts a View from Every Room

No. 90202

Here's a handsome, three-bedroom home with a wide-open feeling. The central entry opens to an L-shaped living and dining room arrangement. Both rooms benefit from the toasty warmth of the living room fireplace and sliders to the upper terrace. The kitchen adjoins a sunny nook, which overlooks both the backyard and the family room below. Step down to the garage level, which includes the rustic, fireplaced family room, powder room, and laundry room. Bedrooms are a short staircase up from the entry. The front bedrooms share a full bath, but the master suite features its own private bath, dressing room, and balcony.

Main level — 728 sq. ft.
Lower level — 310 sq. ft.
Upper level — 874 sq. ft.
Garage — 2-car

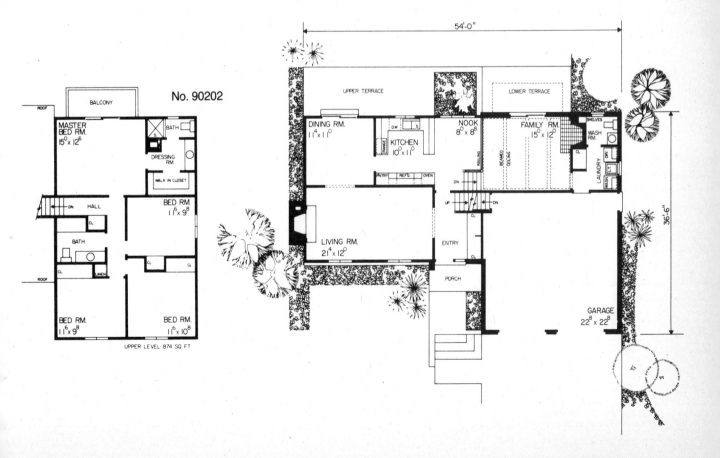

Great Traffic Pattern Highlights Home

No. 90901

Victorian styling and economical construction techniques make this a doubly charming design. This is a compact charmer brimming with features: a sheltered entry leading to the two-story foyer; an island kitchen with convenient pass-through to the formal dining room; a cozy living room brightened by a bay window; an airy central hall upstairs surrounded by large bedrooms with plenty of closet space. And look at that lovely master suite with its sitting area in a bay window.

Main floor — 948 sq. ft.
Second floor — 823 sq. ft.
Basement — 940 sq. ft.
Garage — 440 sq. ft.
Width — 54 ft.
Depth — 33 ft.

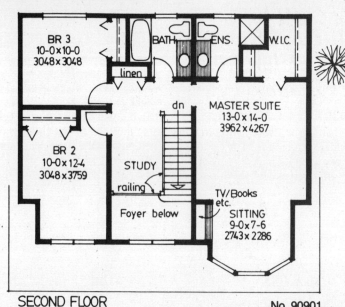

SECOND FLOOR — No. 90901

BR 3
10-0 x 10-0
3048 x 3048

BATH   ENS.   W.I.C.

linen

dn

MASTER SUITE
13-0 x 14-0
3962 x 4267

BR 2
10-0 x 12-4
3048 x 3759

STUDY

railing

Foyer below

TV/Books etc.

SITTING
9-0 x 7-6
2743 x 2286

PATIO

DOUBLE GARAGE
19-6 x 21-0
5943 x 6400

Lav.

NOOK
7-4 x 12-4
2235 x 3759

KITCHEN
7-6 x 12-4
2286 x 3759

FAMILY ROOM
13-0 x 12-4
3962 x 3759

R

D   W   F

BUFFET

Pass-thru

PANTRY   BRM

dn

DINING
10-0 x 12-4
3048 x 3759

LIVINGROOM
13-0 x 17-10
3962 x 5435

FOYER   up
open over

If built with optional single garage width will be 46'-0"

PORCH

Sloped Ceiling Attractive Feature Of Ranch Design

No. 10548

The fireplace and sloped ceiling in the family room offer something a bit out of the ordinary in a small home. The master bedroom is complete with a full bath with a shower and a dressing area. Bedrooms two and three share a full bath across the hall and a half bath is conveniently located adjacent to the kitchen. A walk-out bay window is shown in the spacious breakfast room, and a bay window with window seat has been designed in the master bedroom. The screened porch off of the breakfast room is an inviting feature for meals outside.

First floor—1,688 sq. ft.
Basement—1,688 sq. ft.
Screened porch—120 sq. ft.
Garage—489 sq. ft.

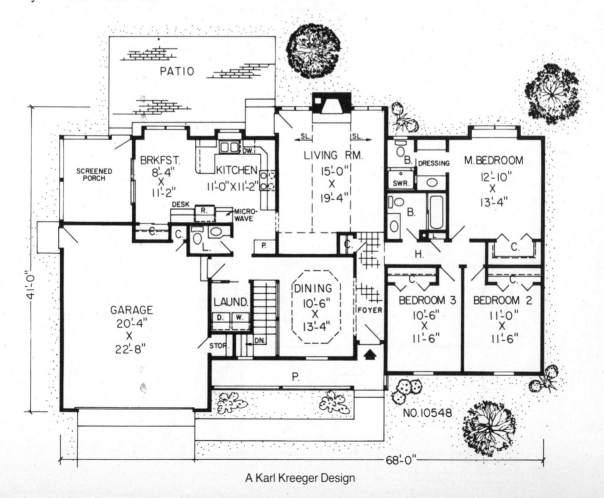

A Karl Kreeger Design

Charming and Cozy Rooms

No. 90126

Here a home that balances both individual and family needs. The traditional design encloses ample space for a large family, while preserving areas for comfort and quiet. The large family room, with cozy fireplace and sliding doors to the patio, is far away from the living room to simplify entertaining. Complementing the formal dining room is an eat-in nook. The efficiently organized kitchen serves either area well. Upstairs, the master bedroom has a large walk-in closet. Two other berooms are nearby for nighttime security.

first floor — 1,260 sq. ft.
Second floor — 952 sq. ft.

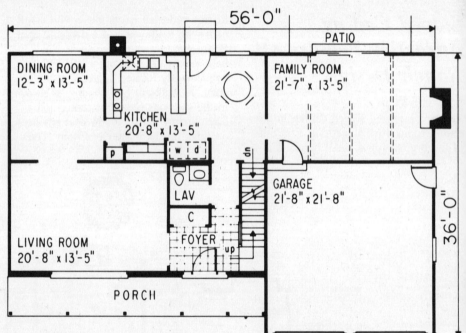

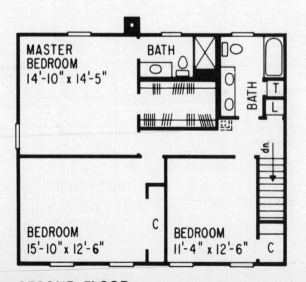

SECOND FLOOR

Contemporary Drama in a Compact Space

No. 91207

Dramatic diagonals add high impact to interior and exterior alike in this four-bedroom contemporary. Imagine the nighttime effect of the illuminated glass-walled staircase. Every bedroom boasts huge closets and sloping ceilings. And, double sinks give the upstairs baths added convenience. You'll love the soaring living room off the foyer, with its cozy fireplace and adjacent screened porch. The nearby dining room overlooks a rear deck. Accessible through french doors in the breakfast nook off the U-shaped kitchen, it's a perfect spot for a casual lunch.

First floor — 930 sq. ft.
Second floor — 1,362 sq. ft.
Garage and storage — 568 sq. ft.
Basement — 635 sq. ft.

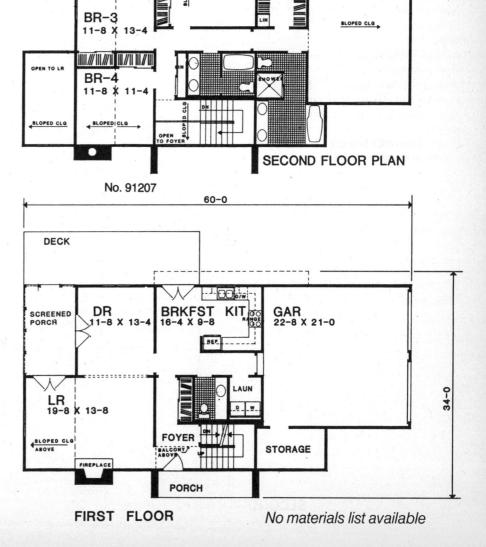

No. 91207

SECOND FLOOR PLAN

BR-2 13-0 X 11-8
MBR 15-8 X 21-0
BR-3 11-8 X 13-4
BR-4 11-8 X 11-4
WALK-IN CLOSET
SLOPED CLG
OPEN TO LR
OPEN TO FOYER

FIRST FLOOR

60-0
34-0

DECK
SCREENED PORCH
DR 11-8 X 13-4
BRKFST 16-4 X 9-8
KIT
GAR 22-8 X 21-0
LAUN
LR 19-8 X 13-8
FOYER
STORAGE
FIREPLACE
PORCH

No materials list available

Colonial Charmer Fit for a Crowd

No. 20101

Imagine entertaining in this spacious masterpiece! Throw open the double doors between the front parlor and fire-placed family room and you've got an expansive room that can handle any crowd. There's room for an army of cooks in the bayed kitchen-breakfast room combination. And, when the oven overheats the room, head out to the adjoining deck for a breath of fresh air. Store extra supplies in the room-sized pantry on the way to the elegant, formal dining room. The adjacent breezeway contains a handy powder room and laundry facilities. Four bedrooms are tucked upstairs, away from the action. Look at the magnificent master suite. Recessed ceilings, a skylit shower, and double vanities make this room both luxurious and convenient.

First floor — 1,109 sq. ft.
Second floor — 932 sq. ft.
Basement — 1,109 sq. ft.
Garage — 552 sq. ft.

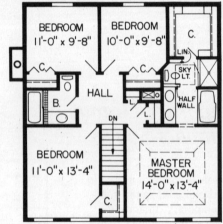

SECOND FLOOR

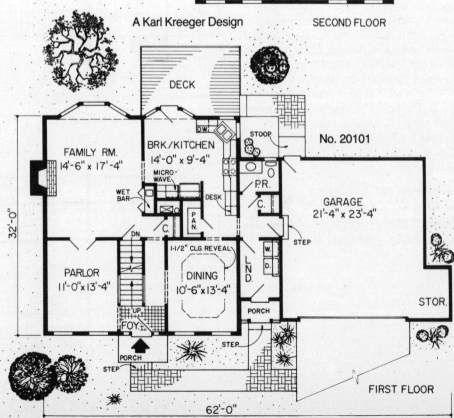

A Karl Kreeger Design

No. 20101

FIRST FLOOR

Affordable Energy-Saver Loaded with Amenities

No. 90680

This attractive ranch, which possesses many features only available in larger homes, is the perfect choice for the budget-conscious family looking for a touch of luxury. Look at the wide-open arrangement of the living and dining rooms, bathed in light from skylights overhead and large expanses of front and rear-facing glass. A heat circulating fireplace helps lower your energy bills. Enjoy your morning coffee in the greenhouse setting of the dinette bay off the kitchen. Or, on a summer morning, the terrace off the dining room is a nice place to spread out with the Sunday paper. In the bedroom wing off the foyer lie three bedrooms, served by two full baths. Look at the private deck complete with hot tub off the master suite.

Living area — 1,393 sq. ft.
Basement — 1,393 sq. ft.
Garage-laundry — 542 sq. ft.
Front porch — 195 sq. ft.

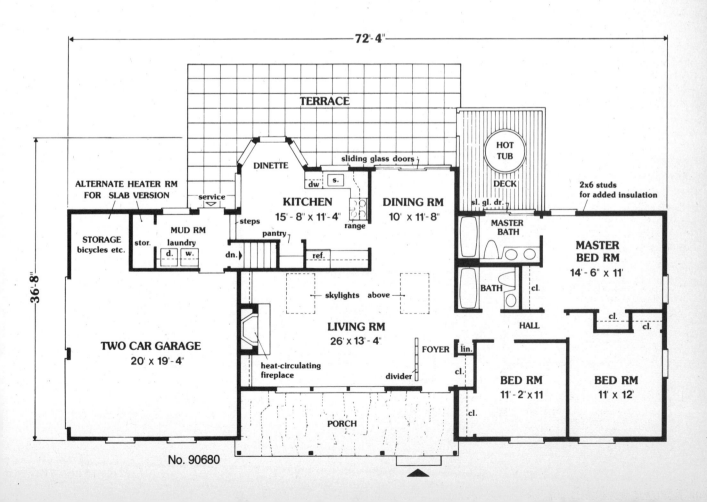

Floor Plan — Second Floor

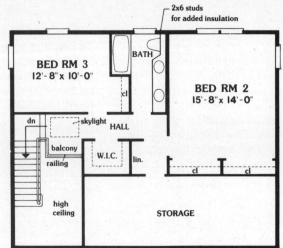

2x6 studs
for added insulation

BED RM 3
12'-8" x 10'-0"

BATH

cl

BED RM 2
15'-8" x 14'-0"

dn

skylight

HALL

balcony

railing

W.I.C.

lin.

cl

cl

high
ceiling

STORAGE

First Floor Master Suite is Special

No. 90624

American as apple pie, this three-bedroom Colonial classic has a welcoming warmth that will capture your fancy. The two-story foyer is lit from above by a skylight. Special features abound throughout the house: access the terrace or garage through the family room, a convenient kitchen which serves family and formal dining areas with ease, and a heatcirculating fireplace flanked by shelves in the living room. The spacious master suite, housed in a separate wing, has vaulted ceilings and is illuminated by spectacular windows on three walls. With a whirlpool tub and its own entertainment center, this room is bound to be your favorite retreat.

Living area — 1,973 sq. ft.
Basement — 1,340 sq. ft.

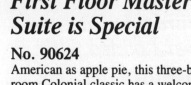

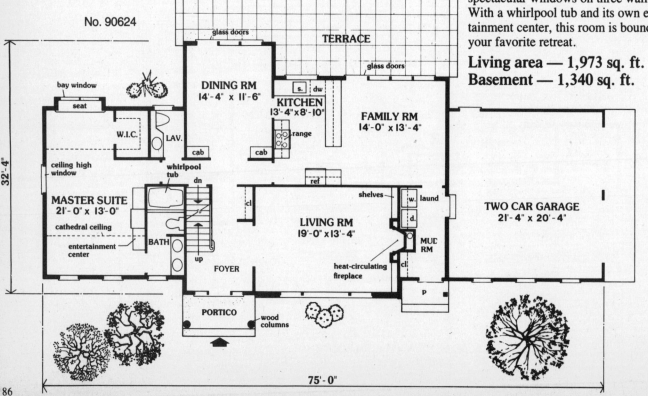

No. 90624

glass doors

TERRACE

glass doors

bay window

seat

DINING RM
14'-4" x 11'-6"

s.

dw

KITCHEN
13'-4" x 8'-10"

FAMILY RM
14'-0" x 13'-4"

W.I.C.

LAV.

range

cab

cab

ceiling high
window

whirlpool
tub

dn

ref

shelves

w.

laund

TWO CAR GARAGE
21'-4" x 20'-4"

32'-4"

MASTER SUITE
21'-0" x 13'-0"

cathedral ceiling

entertainment
center

BATH

cl

up

LIVING RM
19'-0" x 13'-4"

d.

MUD
RM

FOYER

heat-circulating
fireplace

cl

p

PORTICO

wood
columns

75'-0"

Zoned for Comfort

No. 90610

This ground-hugging ranch was designed for maximum use of three basic living areas. The informal area — fireplaced family room, kitchen, and breakfast room — adjoins a covered porch. The fully-equipped kitchen is easily accessible to the formal dining room, which flows into the living room for convenient entertaining. Well-situated closets and bathrooms set the bedrooms apart from more active areas. The spacious master suite includes plenty of closet space and its own bath. The other bedrooms are served by the lavish hall bath equipped with two basins.

Basic house — 1,771 sq. ft.

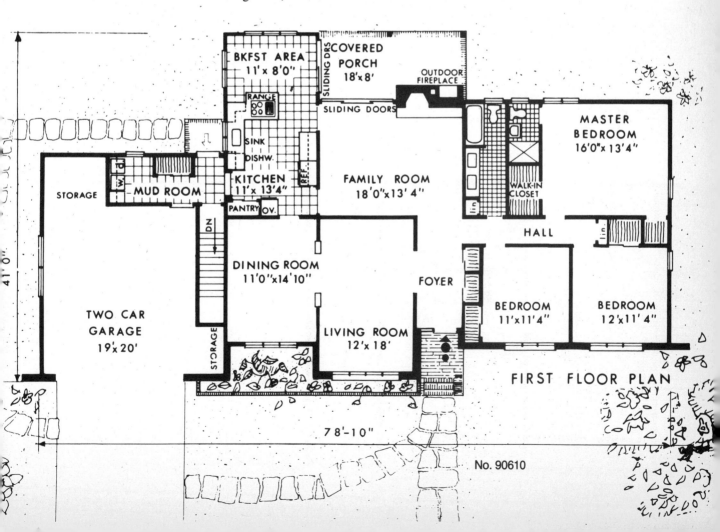

FIRST FLOOR PLAN

No. 90610

A Tudor-style Gem

No. 90172

A private, sheltered stairway leads to your comfortable retreat over this two car garage plan. Designed to provide secure storage for recreational vehicles or boats while you're away, these plans are becoming increasingly popular thanks to their affodability and style. Beautifully designed, the living space includes room for washer and dryer, a full bath with tub, a handy kitchen, an optional deck off the dining area, a separate entry space, suprisingly roomy living room, and good-sized bedroom. Tudor accents on the exterior lend a touch of class to a structure that will give you peace of mind while you're away.

Living Area — 784 sq. ft.
Garage — 784 sq. ft.

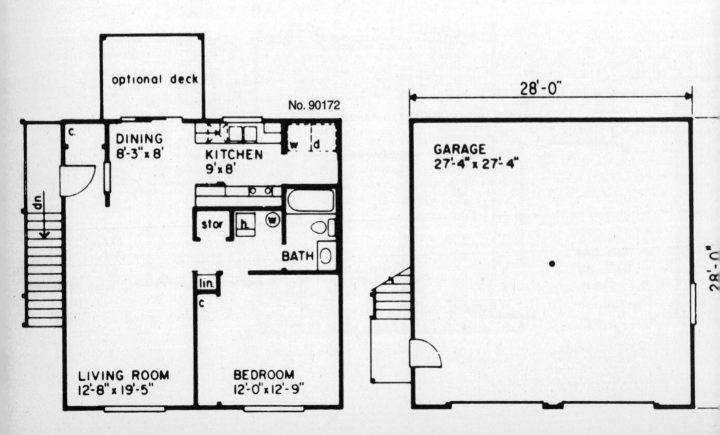

Light, Airy, and Easy-Care

No. 91218

Here's a convenient plan with a wide-open feeling. Walk up the stairs from the foyer and survey the spacious, two-story living room below, heated by a massive fireplace that will warm the whole house. Convenient features upstairs include double sinks in the skylit master bath, a handy chute that delivers dirty clothes right to the laundry facilities, and a full bath and dressing room adjoining the other bedrooms. Downstairs, you'll marvel at the step-saving layout of the island kitchen that serves the formal dining room, breakfast room, and screened porch with ease.

First floor — 945 sq. ft.
Second floor — 1,108 sq. ft.
Screened porch — 106 sq. ft.
Garage — 484 sq. ft.

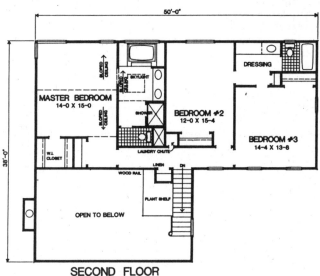

SECOND FLOOR

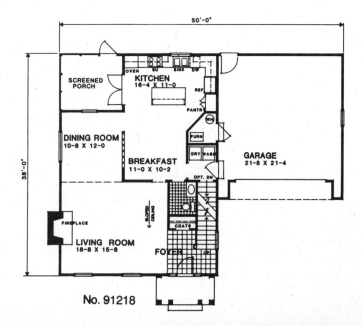

No. 91218

No materials list available

Cozy Window Seat Commands Front Yard View

No. 90517

From the covered front porch to the deck off the breakfast nook, this country home is surrounded by outdoor living space. Designed for easy traffic flow, the first floor revolves around a central staircase. Living, dining, and fireplaced family rooms are graced by huge windows. For formal entertaining, a door separates guests in the dining room from the bustling activity of the kitchen. Three bedrooms and two full baths are tucked upstairs.

First floor — 1,065 sq. ft.
Second floor — 813 sq. ft.

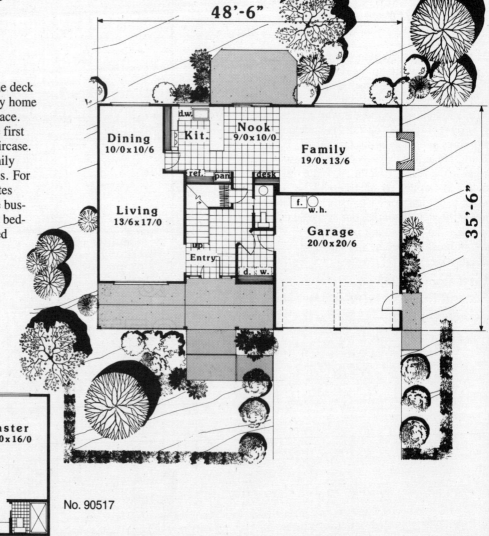

No. 90517

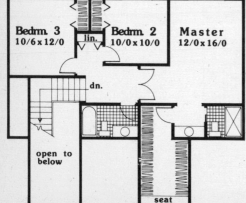

Clever Touches Improve Design

No. 20061

A lot can be said about this unique design. Its exterior of vertical siding, shake shingle and rock, and the large round picture window set this design apart. The interior is delightfully planned beginning with the kitchen that has a built-in pantry, refrigerator, dishwasher and range. In addition, the kitchen has a breakfast bar, an open-beamed ceiling with a skylight, plus a breakfast area with lots of windows. A very formal dining room is partitioned from the living room. The living room has two open beams running down a sloping ceiling, and a fireplace. There is a laundry closet and the foyer area also has a closet. Three bedrooms share a full bath. The master bedroom has an open-beamed, sloping ceiling with a spacious bath area and a walk-in closet.

First floor — 1,667 sq. ft.
Basement — 1,657 sq. ft.
Garage — 472 sq. ft.

A Karl Kreeger Design

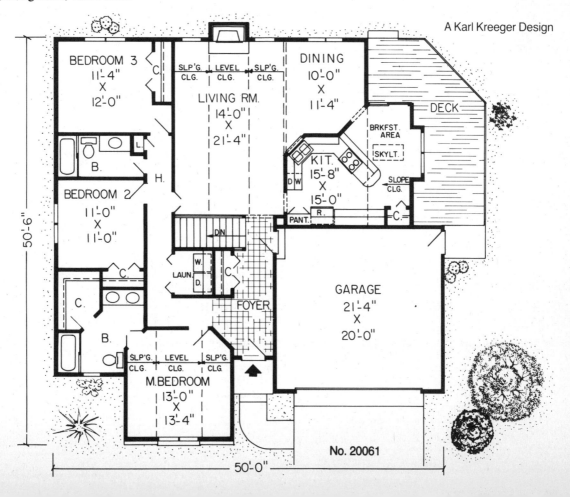

Graceful Porch Enhances Charm

No. 90106

The formal living room which is sheltered by the railed porch may be used only for company because of the multifunctional kitchen, dining and family room which are immediately behind it. This "three rooms in one" design is eas-ily adaptable to any number of lifestyles. Adjacent to the open kitchen with its efficient design and ample counter space is the hobby area that includes laundry facilities. Of the three large bedrooms the master bedroom features a walk-in closet and private bath.

Living Area — 1,643 sq. ft.

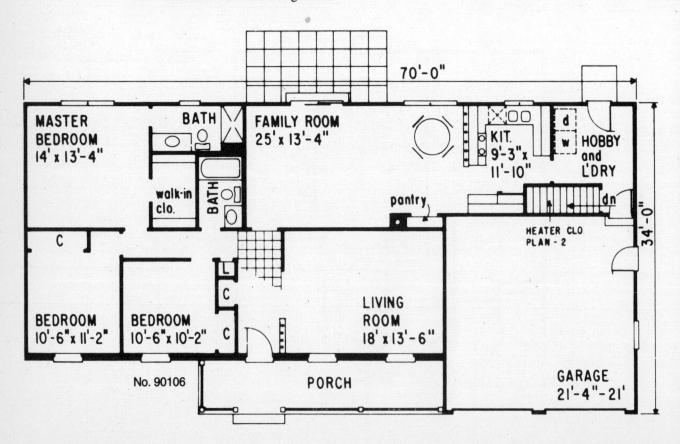

Attractive and Functional

No. 90259

This classic, split-entry plan stacks living areas for affordable construction. Step down from the central entry to the garage level, where you'll find a huge, fire-placed family room, study or fourth bed-room, laundry, and full bath. Or step up to an open living and dining room arrangement with access to a raised out-door deck. Eat in formal elegance, or in the breakfast nook off the U-shaped kitchen. Three bedrooms and two full baths, tucked down a hallway over the garage, include the master suite with private dressing room and twin vanities.

Upper level — 1,456 sq. ft.
Lower level — 728 sq. ft.
Garage — 2-car

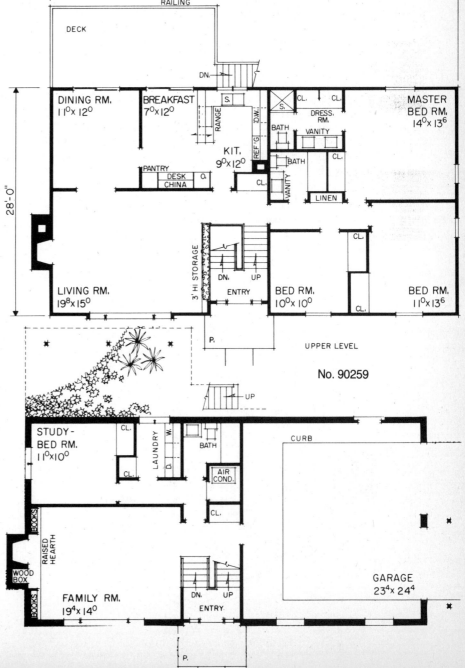

Glass Captures Views & Sun

No. 90121

Abundant glass floods this plan with light and offers images of the surrounding scenery from three sides, as well as serving as a solar energy feature. Large exterior exposed beams crisscross the glass giving a massive, rugged appearance. The center of family activity begins in the family room and proceeds to the deck which flows into a dining patio on the left side. Your family may relax over meals here or in the dining/kitchen area just inside glass doors. Two bedrooms, a full bath and laundry facilities complete the first level. An open wooden stairway beckons you to the second level which opens into a large fireplaced sitting room and balcony overlooking the family room.

First floor — 1,126 sq. ft.
Second floor — 603 sq. ft.

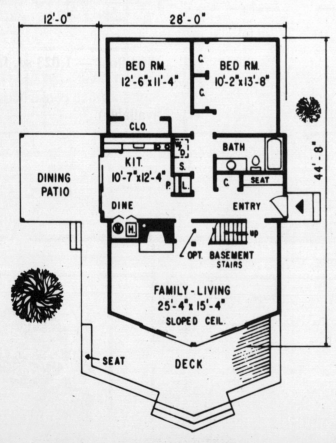

FIRST FLOOR

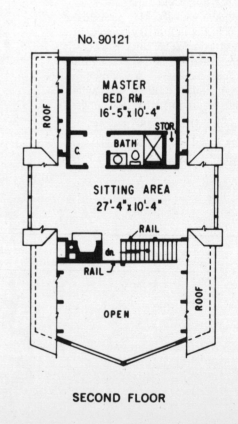

SECOND FLOOR

Traditional Elements Combine in Friendly Colonial

No. 90606

Casual living is the theme of this elegant Farmhouse Colonial. A beautiful circular stair ascends from the central foyer, flanked by the formal living and dining rooms. The informal family room, accessible from the foyer, captures the Early American style with exposed beams, wood paneling, and brick fireplace wall. A separate dinette opens to an efficient kitchen.

First floor — 1,023 sq. ft.
Second floor — 923 sq. ft.
(optional slab construction available)

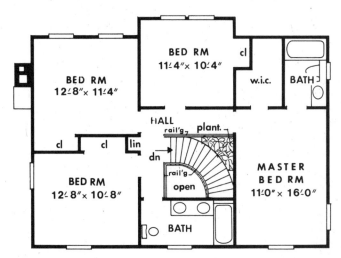

BED RM
11'-4" x 10'-4"   cl

BED RM
12'-8" x 11'-4"   w.i.c.   BATH

cl   cl   lin

HALL
rail'g   plant.

dn

BED RM
12'-8" x 10'-8"   rail'g   open   MASTER BED RM
11'-0" x 16'-0"

BATH

No. 90606

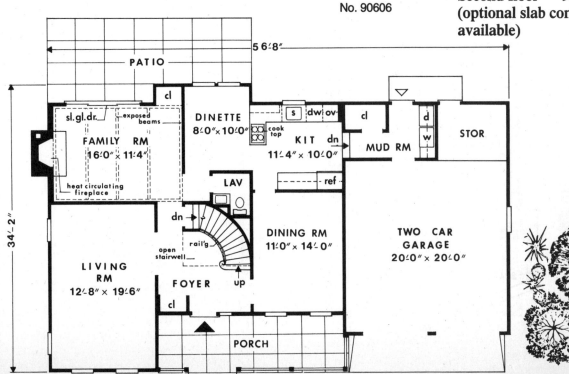

56'-8"

PATIO   cl

sl. gl. dr.   exposed beams   DINETTE
8'-0" x 10'-0"   s   dw   ov   cl   d   STOR

FAMILY RM
16'-0" x 11'-4"   cook top   KIT
11'-4" x 10'-0"   dn   MUD RM   w

heat circulating fireplace   ref

LAV

dn   rail'g   DINING RM
11'-0" x 14'-0"   TWO CAR GARAGE
20'-0" x 20'-0"

LIVING RM
12'-8" x 19'-6"   open stairwell   up

FOYER

cl

34'-2"

PORCH

Mountain Retreat

No. 10751

Relax and enjoy this compact vacation home. With vertical cedar siding, you won't need to expend much energy on exterior upkeep. The central entry opens right into the living room, a warm and spacious center of activity. Serve meals right over the counter in the galley kitchen. The main floor bedroom and full bath make one-floor living an inviting option. Save the stairs for the guests, unless you want to take advantage of the view from the balcony!

First floor — 660 sq. ft.
Second floor — 330 sq. ft.

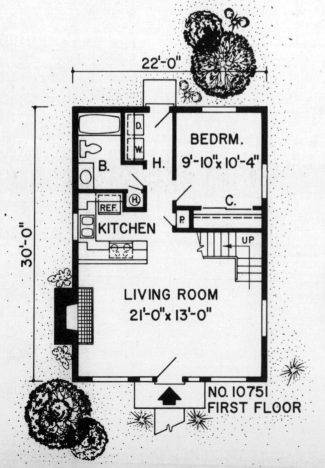

NO. 10751
FIRST FLOOR

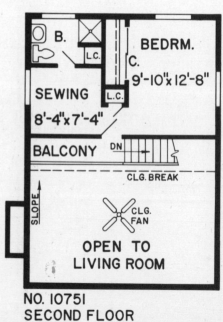

NO. 10751
SECOND FLOOR

No. 10751

An Asset to Any Neighborhood

No. 90556

With abundant rear-facing windows, this clapboard classic takes full advantage of a beautiful backyard view. And, interior views are just as exciting. From the angular staircase, you can look down over the fireplaced living and dining rooms, or glance up at the balcony hall that links four bedrooms and two full baths. A desk in the back bedroom, twin vanities in the master bath, and a cozy window seat in the front bedroom add convenience and help cut clutter. You'll find the same efficient approach in active areas, with built-ins in the fireplaced family room, a pantry tucked under the stairs in the U-shaped kitchen, and the side-by-side arrangement of powder and laundry rooms just behind the garage.

First floor — 1,055 sq. ft.
Second floor — 1,030 sq. ft.
Garage — 2-car

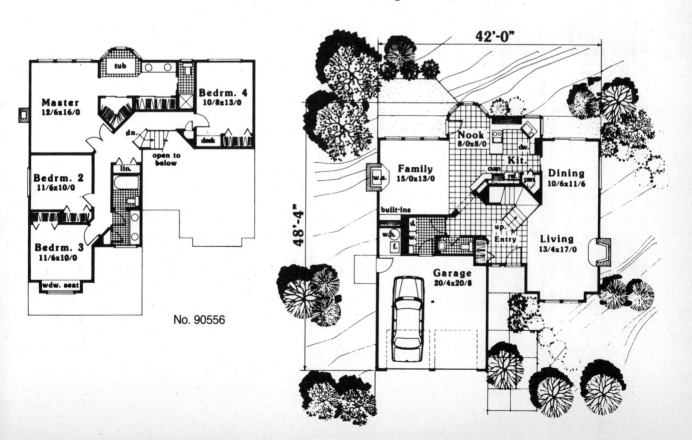

No. 90556

Ranch Incorporates Victorian Features

No. 20058

This wonderful Victorian-featured ranch design incorporates many luxury conveniences usually offered in larger designs. The master bedroom is expansive in size, with an oversized full bath complete with a walk-in closet, an individual shower, a full tub, and two-sink wash basin. A large kitchen area is offered with a built-in island for convenience. The kitchen also has its own breakfast area. Located next to the kitchen is a half bath. The living area is separated from the dining room by a half-partition wall. Two large bedrooms complete the interior of the house. They have large closets and share a full bath. A two-car garage and a wood deck complete the options listed in this design.

First floor — 1,787 sq. ft.
Basement — 1,787 sq. ft.
Garage — 484 sq. ft.

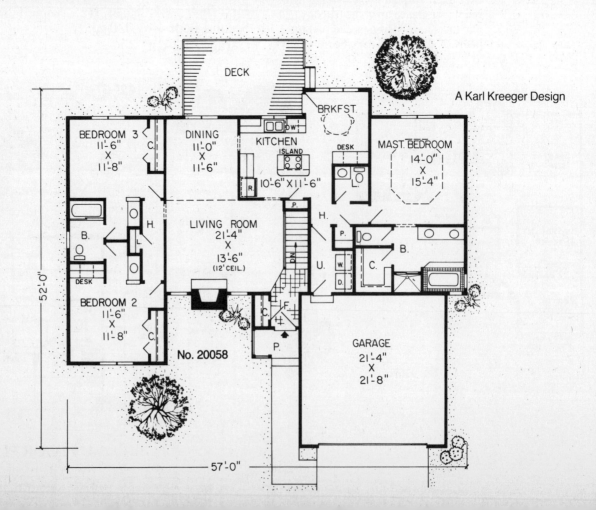

A Karl Kreeger Design

Built-In Entertainment Center for Family Fun

No. 90615

Up-to-date features bring this center hall colonial into the 20th century. The focus of the Early American living room is a heat-circulating fireplace, framed by decorative pilasters that support dropped beams. Both dining areas open to the rear terrace through sliding glass doors. And, the convenient mud room provides access to the two car garage. Four bedrooms and two baths, including the spacious master suite, occupy the second floor.

**Total living area — 1,973 sq. ft.
Garage — 441 sq. ft.
(optional slab construction available)**

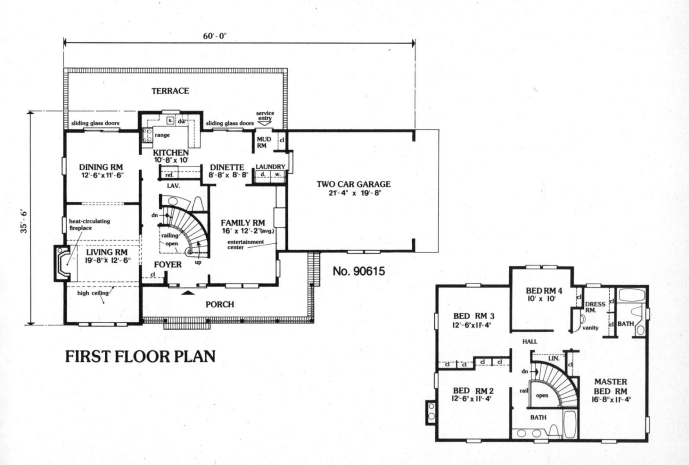

FIRST FLOOR PLAN

SECOND FLOOR PLAN

Brick Home Features Unified Floor Plan

No. 90103

From the sheltering porch, through the foyer and into the spacious living area, this home will make quite an impression. The central kitchen and dining areas separate the two smaller bedrooms from the master bedroom which is insulated from the street noise by the garage. The laundry area is conveniently located in the utility and storage area.

Living area — 1,494 sq. ft.

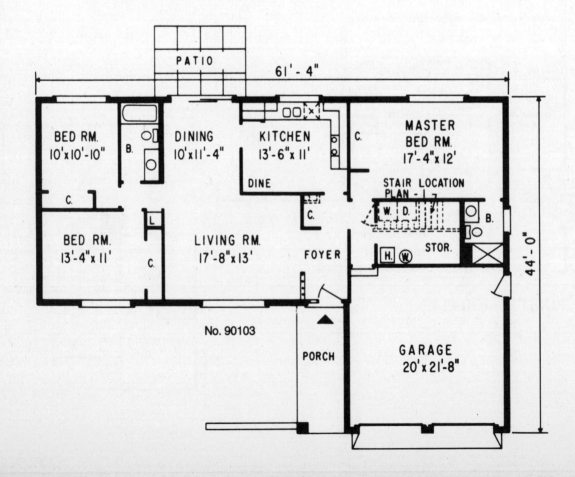

Compact Dream House

No. 90245

Does your building lot have a small buildable area? Here's a compact Cape that can fit in the smallest space, and still fulfill the dreams of your growing family. The central entry is flanked by a cozy study and a sunny, formal living room with windows on two sides. Two fireplaces help with the heating bills, adding a friendly glow to active areas. Eat in the formal dining room, or in the huge country kitchen, which features a triple window with built-in seating and a beamed ceiling. Three bedrooms share the second floor with two full baths. You'll love the cheerful atmosphere upstairs, achieved by generous windows and a full dormer overlooking the backyard.

First floor — 1,020 sq. ft.
Second floor — 777 sq. ft.

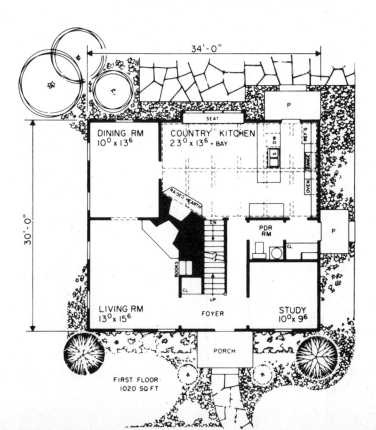

FIRST FLOOR
1020 SQ FT

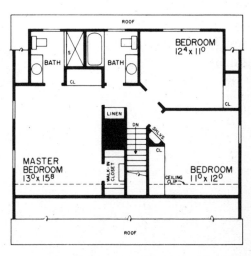

SECOND FLOOR - 777 SQ. FT.

No. 90245

Split-level Made for Growing Family

No. 10524

The entry-level living room features a fireplace and, just a few steps up, a dining room which overlooks the living room and adjoins the kitchen. The efficient kitchen features an eat-in space and sliding-door access to the deck. Three bedrooms, two baths, and a convenient laundry room comprise the rest of the upper floor. The fourth bedroom, with its own bath, could be used as a guest room or to give more privacy to the teenager in the family. There's also a cozy family room and plenty of storage in the basement.

Upper floor — 1,470 sq. ft.
Lower floor — 711 sq. ft.
Basement — 392 sq. ft.
Garage — 563 sq. ft.

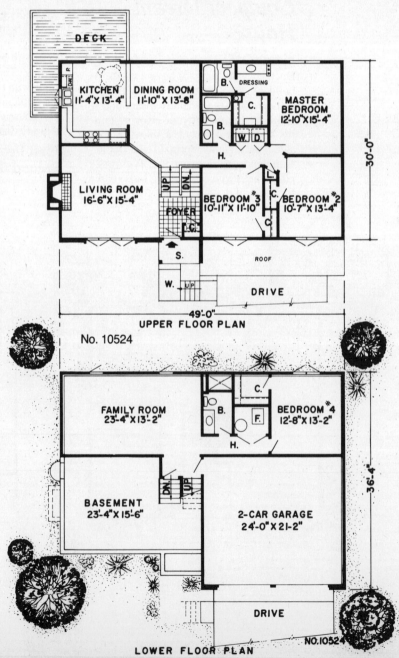

A Karl Kreeger Design

Victorian Touches Disguise Modern Design

No. 90616

Indulge in the romance of Victorian styling without sacrificing up-to-date living. Out of the past come porches with turned wood posts, exterior walls of round shingles, wonderful bay windows, and decorative scroll work. But the present is evident in the kitchen and family room, with a skylit entertainment area for today's electronic pleasures. The stairs begins its rise with a turned post and rail. The master suite features a high ceiling with an arched window, private bath, and tower sitting room with adjoining roof deck.

Basic house - 1,956 sq. ft.
Laundry — 36 sq. ft.
Garage — 440 sq. ft.
Basement — 967 sq. ft.

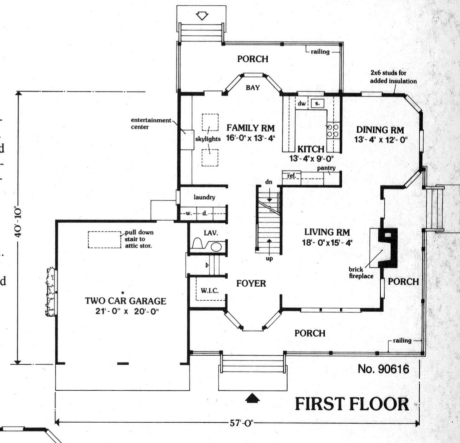

FIRST FLOOR

No. 90616

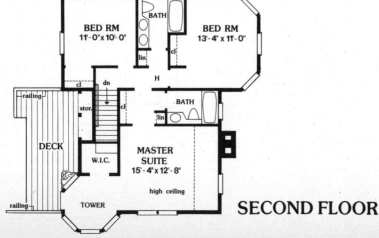

SECOND FLOOR

Fireplaces Warm Roomy Ranch

No. 90908

Here's a delightful one-level home you can build for a bargain. Save foundation costs with this no-basement design. Also, note that careful planning has placed laundry across from the family bath to eliminate extra plumbing. A wide covered porch shelters the front entry. You'll fall in love with the skylit foyer which provides easy access to all points of this plan. The formal areas are well separated from the family areas. The kitchen, nook, and family rooms form plenty of casual living space. Beyond the nook through sliding glass doors is an ideal location for future deck or grade level patio.

Total living area — 1,499 sq. ft.
Garage — 452 sq. ft.
Width — 42 ft.
Depth — 51 ft.

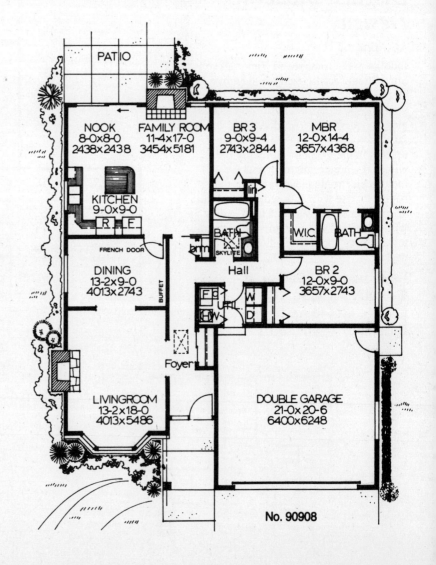

No. 90908

Vertical Siding Adds Contemporary Appeal

No. 91407

Here's a traditional family home with a contemporary flavor. The entry is flanked by the dramatic, vaulted living room and a cozy den that doubles as a guest room. Informal areas at the rear of the house command an expansive view of the back yard, thanks to windows on three sides. And, the unique, open arrangement of the rangetop island kitchen, dining bay, and fireplaced family room keeps the cook from getting lonely. The U-shaped stairs, just across from the handy powder room, lead to a balcony linking three bedrooms. You'll love the master suite, which features a luxurious sunken tub with a view. Need more room? Finish the optional bonus space over the garage. Specify a crawl-space or basement when ordering this plan.

First floor — 1,153 sq. ft.
Second floor — 787 sq. ft.
Garage — 537 sq. ft.

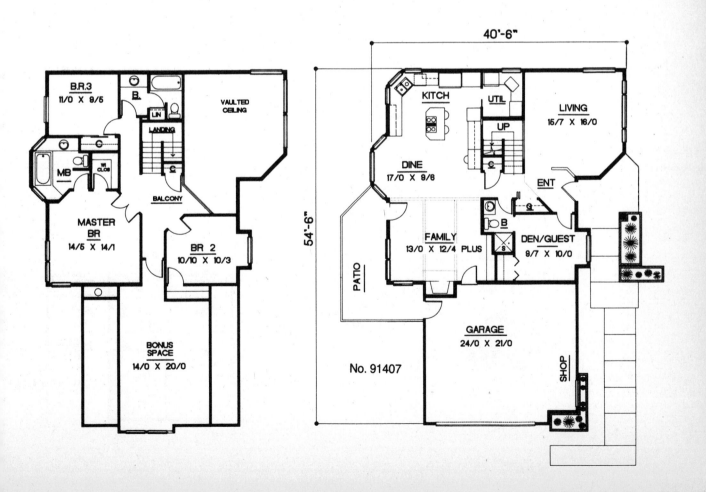

Gingerbread Charm

No. 10690

Victorian elegance combines with a modern floor plan to make this a dream house without equal. A wrap-around porch and rear deck add lots of extra living space to the roomy first floor, which features a formal parlor and dining room just off the central entry. Informal areas at the rear of the house are wide-open for family interaction. Gather the crew around the fireplace in the family room, or make supper in the kitchen while you supervise the kids' homework in the sunwashed breakfast room. Three bedrooms, tucked upstairs for a quiet atmosphere, feature skylit baths. And, you'll love the five-sided sitting nook in your master suite, a perfect spot to relax after a luxurious bath in the sunken tub.

First floor — 1,260 sq. ft.
Second floor — 1,021 sq. ft.
Basement — 1,186 sq. ft.
Garage — 840 sq. ft.

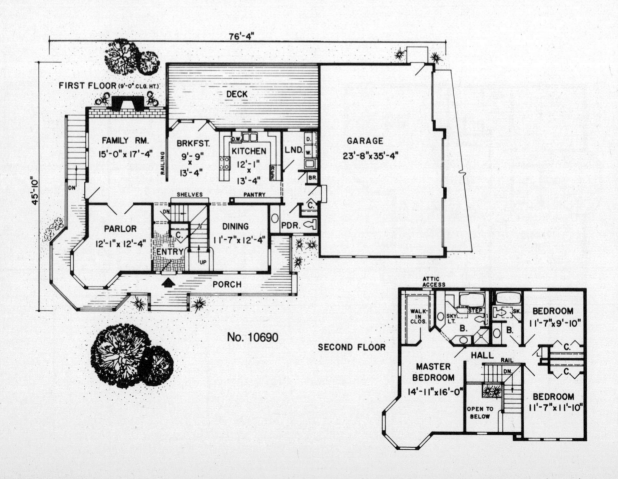

No. 10690

Place This House For Solar Gain

No. 90620

This modest ranch with generous rooms and passive solar features provides comfortable living for the family on a budget. The soaring, skylit central foyer provides access to every room. Straight ahead, the living room, dining room, and greenhouse form a bright, airy arrangement of glass and open space. The adjacent kitchen conveniently opens to a spacious, bay-windowed dinette. A separate wing contains three bedrooms and two baths, including an ample master suite.

Total living area — 1,405 sq. ft.
Basement — 1,415 sq. ft.

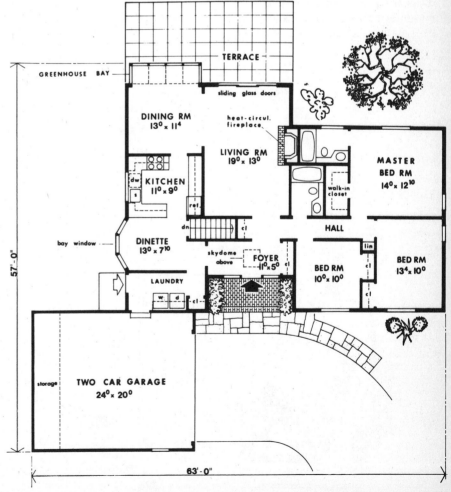

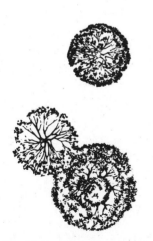

No. 90620

Master Retreat Crowns Compact Castle

No. 90552

An angular entry provides a covered approach for guests entering this four-bedroom, Tudor-influenced classic. With its huge, leaded glass window and soaring ceilings, the sunken living room is contemporary, yet touched with an old English flavor. Coupled with the formal dining room right across the entry, this is an ideal spot for entertaining. And, serving your guests couldn't be easier, with the efficient kitchen just steps away. Imagine the cozy atmosphere in the family room, which features a sunny bay for informal meals, and access to a rear deck. Three bedrooms, served by a full bath at the top of the stairs, share the second floor with the master suite.

First floor — 983 sq. ft.
Second floor — 927 sq. ft.
Garage — 2-car

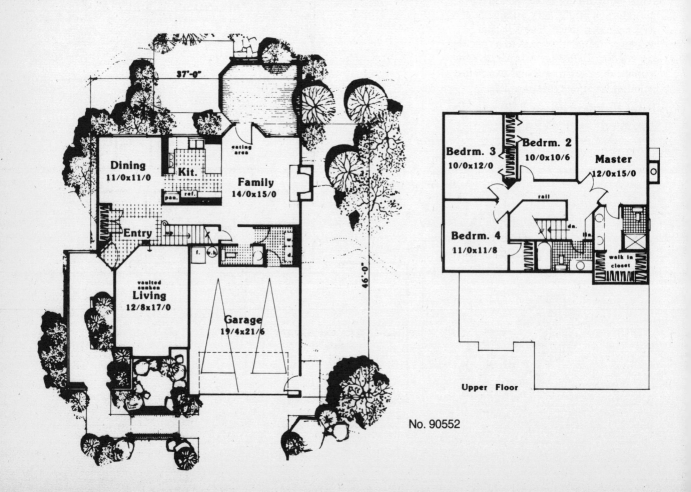

No. 90552

Comfortable Contemporary

No. 90392

Fieldstone and rough-sawn siding lend a rustic feeling to this cheerful, contemporary classic. The entry, flooded with natural light from clerestory windows overhead, opens to a two-story living with a view of the second-floor balcony. Step up the open staircase to four, sunny bedrooms. You'll love the master suite, which features a private bath with both tub and walk-in shower. Just off the living room, the formal dining room at the rear of the house is served by a spacious, efficient kitchen any cook would covet. And, the sunken, fireplaced family room just past the breakfast nook invites you to take your shoes off and get comfortable!

First floor — 1,237 sq. ft.
Second floor — 1,008 sq. ft.
Garage — 2-car

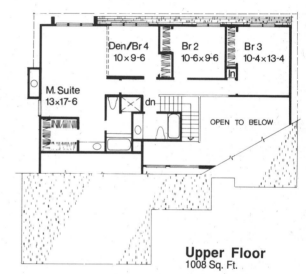

Upper Floor
1008 Sq. Ft.

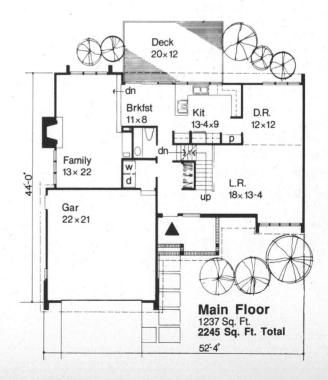

Main Floor
1237 Sq. Ft.
2245 Sq. Ft. Total

No. 90392

Relaxed and Economical Living

No. 21126

Well suited for the economy-minded small family or as a second home, this design is sure to please. To the left of a large front entry lies the living room, with deck access, a fireplace and a cathedral ceiling with exposed beams. The living room flows through an eating bar to the kitchen/dining area beyond. The dining room also adjoins the deck. To the right of the entry are two bedrooms and a full bath. Sliding glass doors and full length windows cloak the entire width of the rear of the house on this level. A touch of elegance is provided by a stairway spiraling to the second floor loft. Clerestory windows draw in the sun and illuminate this quiet, secluded room.

First floor — 1,082 sq. ft.
Loft — 262 sq. ft.

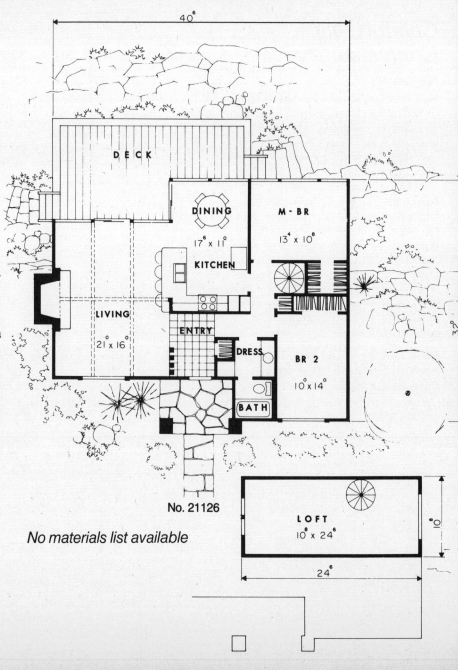

No. 21126

No materials list available

Arched Master Bedroom Window

No. 20055

The arched master bedroom window above the garage gives this three-bedroom, two and a half bath home a special appearance. The spacious kitchen opens onto a deck and adjoins a breakfast room with pantry. The entrance foyer lends access to the living room, formal dining room or stairs. The sloped ceiling in the master bedroom, a large bath with linen closet, dressing area and walk-in closet provide a sense of drama and complete privacy.

First floor — 928 sq. ft.
Second floor — 773 sq. ft.
Garage — 484 sq. ft.
Basement — 910 sq. ft.

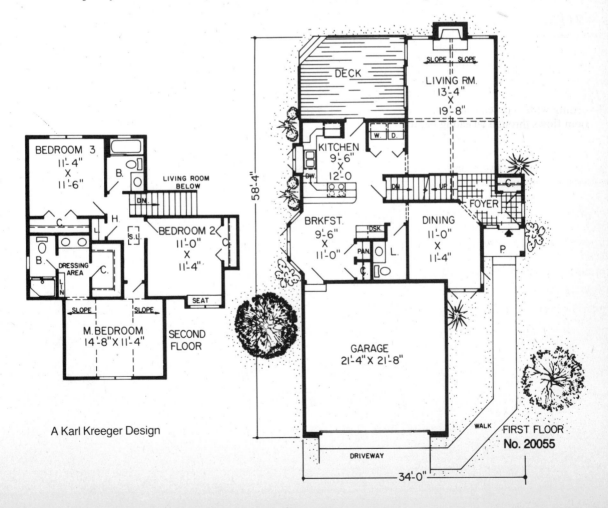

A Karl Kreeger Design

Clerestory Windows
Let the Sun Shine In

No. 90926

A striking contemporary exterior compliments the exceptional floor plan in this attractive ranch home zoned for area function. Designed to sit on a level lot, it could be adapted to a hillside building site. Some of the amenities include a secluded, covered breakfast patio off the family room, a distinctive, angular kitchen, a fireplace complete with wood box, and a vaulted ceiling with clerestory windows in the sunken living room. The master suite features a 3/4 bath and a big walk-in closet.

Main floor — 1,589 sq. ft.
Basement — 1,531 sq. ft.
Garage — 472 sq. ft.
Width — 60 ft.
Depth — 58 ft.

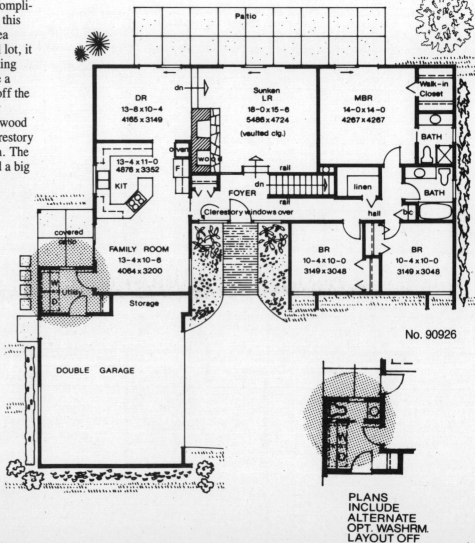

No. 90926

PLANS INCLUDE ALTERNATE OPT. WASHRM. LAYOUT OFF UTILITY

Stacked Sleeping Rooms for Quiet Bedtimes

No. 20069

The kids can sleep in peace, away from the action, in this modern charmer with loft views of the living room and foyer below. Double windows give every room a cheery atmosphere. Soaring ceilings add drama to living and dining rooms, which conveniently flank the open kitchen and breakfast room. And, a deck off the breakfast room provides easy access to outdoor fun. Conveniently situated on the first floor, the master suite is a pleasant retreat.

First floor — 1,313 sq. ft.
Second floor — 588 sq. ft.
Basement — 1,299 sq. ft.

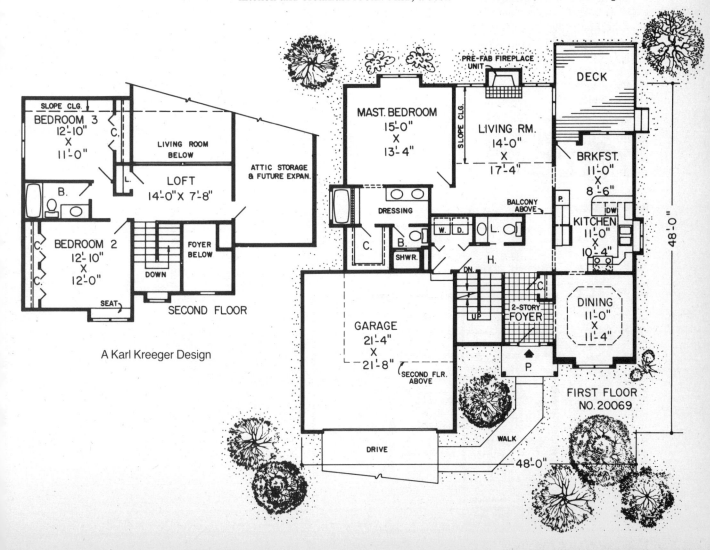

A Karl Kreeger Design

A Hint of Victorian Nostalgia

No. 90909

High roofs, tower bays, and long, railed porches give this efficient plan an old-fashioned charm that's hard to resist. The foyer opens on a classic center stairwell, wrapped in short halls that separate traffic without subtracting from room sizes. The highlight of this home for many homeowners is sure to be the lively kitchen with its full bay window and built-in eating table.

Main floor — 1,206 sq. ft.
Second floor — 969 sq. ft.
Garage — 471 sq. ft.
Unfinished basement —
1,206 sq. ft.
Width — 61 ft.
Depth — 44 ft.

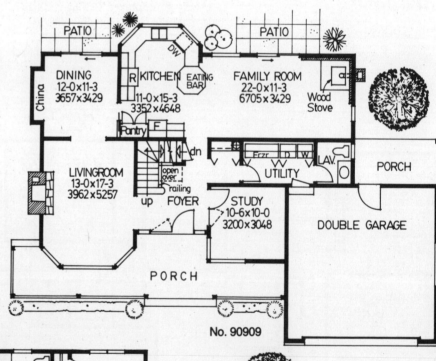

No. 90909

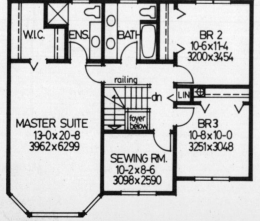

SECOND FLOOR

Sunlight Floods Every Room

No. 90511

Walk into the two-story foyer from the garage or sheltered front entry and you'll be struck by the wide-open spaciousness of this compact home. The kitchen is flanked by vaulted living and dining rooms on one side and a fireplaced fam-ily room and breakfast nook on the other. Atop the open stairs, the plush master bedroom suite lies behind double doors. Two additional bedrooms share an adjoining full bath.

First floor — 1,078 sq. ft.
Second floor — 974 sq. ft.

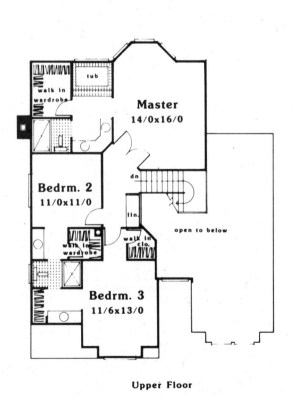

Upper Floor

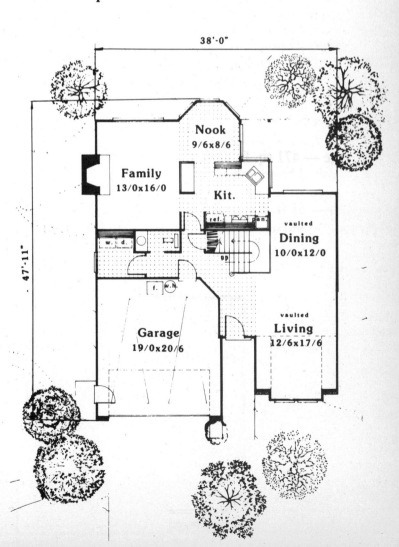

Enjoy the View

No. 90833

Here's a house that will take advantage of your location to create an irresistible view from the second floor. On the lower level, you'll find a bayed family room complete with a fireplace just off the foyer. But, the main living areas are upstairs. The L-shaped staircase brings you right into the living room. Bay windows, the open railing, and adjacent dining area with sliding glass doors to the sundeck give this area a spacious feeling. The family kitchen is large enough to accommodate a table for informal meals. Past the pantry and full bath, three bedrooms occupy the rear of the house, away from active areas and the noise of the street.

Basement floor — 994 sq. ft.
Main floor — 1,318 sq. ft.
Garage — 378 sq. ft.

FLOOR AREA = 1318 sq.ft.
WIDTH: 40'-0"
DEPTH: 40'-0"

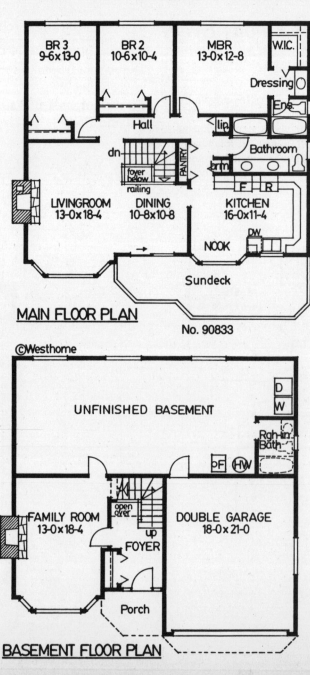

MAIN FLOOR PLAN

No. 90833

BASEMENT FLOOR PLAN

Stacked Windows Hint at Exciting Living Spaces

No. 90543

With a view in every direction, this exceptional home deserves a beautiful location. The vaulted entry, brightened by an arched window high overhead, opens to the soaring spaces of the formal living and dining rooms. Window walls and sliders to the back yard lend a greenhouse feeling to family areas at the rear of the house. Off the entry, just past the laundry and powder rooms, the den doubles as a bedroom if you need an extra. The open staircase leads to three bedrooms, each with a private dressing area and adjoining bath. The master suite, with its double-door entry, raised tub with back yard view, and private sitting bay, is a luxurious retreat you're sure to appreciate.

First floor — 1,283 sq. ft.
Second floor — 1,068 sq. ft.
Garage — 3-car

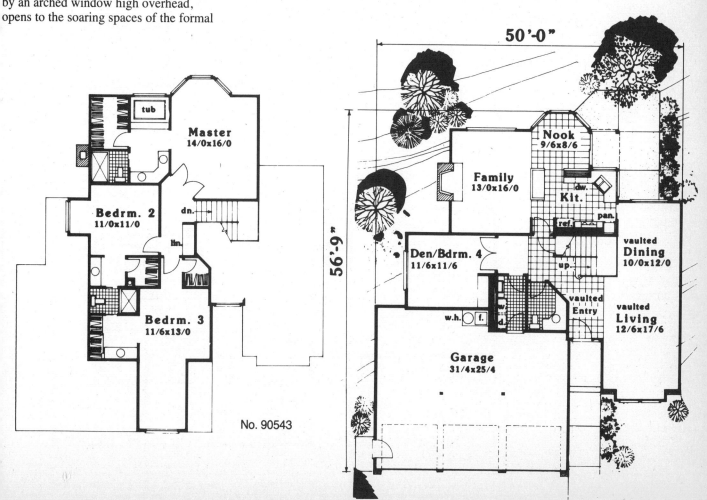

Country Comforts

No. 90687

The farmhouse flavor of a covered porch, window boxes, and two chimneys give this house a welcoming feeling that couldn't be friendlier. And, the interior's just as nice, with the cozy living and dining rooms beckoning guests as they step into the foyer. Cabinets and a greenhouse bay separate the kitchen, dinette, and family room overlooking the backyard without compromising the spacious atmosphere throughout. And, a covered porch just off the fireplaced family room is a great place for a barbecue, rain or shine. Four bedrooms and two full baths are tucked up the circular staircase for privacy. You'll love the luxury of your own whirlpool tub at the end of your busy days.

First floor — 1,065 sq. ft.
Second floor — 1,007 sq. ft.
Laundry-mud room — 88 sq. ft.
Garage — 428 sq. ft.

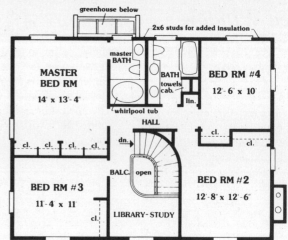

SECOND FLOOR PLAN

No. 90687

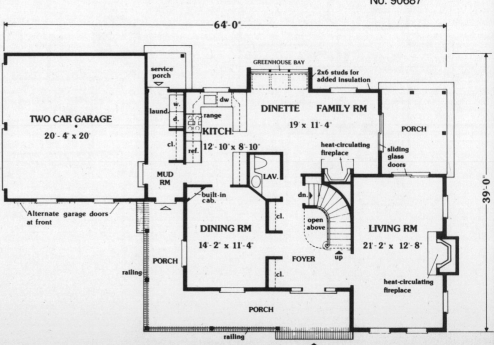

Ranch Offers Attractive Windows

No. 10569

This four bedroom ranch offers two full baths with plenty of closet space. Also in this design, the living room has a sloping, open beamed ceiling with a fireplace and built-in fireplace bookshelves. The dining room is connected to the foyer and has a vaulted ceiling, adding to an already spacious room. The kitchen has an ample amount of dining space available and has sliding glass doors that lead out onto a brick patio. A half-bath with shower is located next to the kitchen as well as a pantry and washer/dryer space for more convenience. A two car garage is available in this plan.

First floor — 1,840 sq. ft.
Basement — 1,803 sq. ft.
Garage — 445 sq. ft.

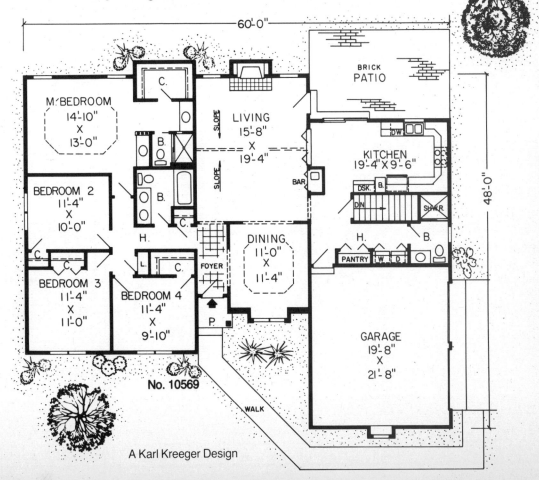

No. 10569

A Karl Kreeger Design

Sheltered Porch Graces Family Dwelling

No. 20067

Consider an easy-to-care-for home if you have a growing family. An all wood exterior that relieves you of yearly maintenance is just one of the features. The compact floor plan minimizes housekeeping yet arranges the play area so that an eye can be kept on young children, whether inside or in the backyard. Note touches like the tiled foyer that stops muddy traffic entering from either the front door or garage. Three bedrooms are located near to one another on the same level for nighttime security. The basement provides room for expansion as the children get older.

Living area — 1,459 sq. ft.
Basement — 697 sq. ft.
Garage — 694 sq. ft.

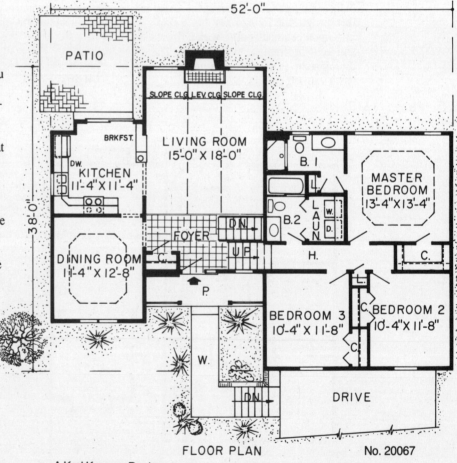

FLOOR PLAN   No. 20067

A Karl Kreeger Design

Overhang Provides Shade from the Noonday Sun

No. 90502

A sheltered entry opens to the airy, fire-placed living and dining room of this one-level, stucco home. Behind double doors, the family room shares a view of the deck with the kitchen and adjoining, bay windowed breakfast nook. The window of the front bedroom, framed by a graceful arch, looks out over its own, private garden. An angular hall leads to the laundry, two additional bedrooms and two full baths.

Floor area — 1,642 sq. ft.

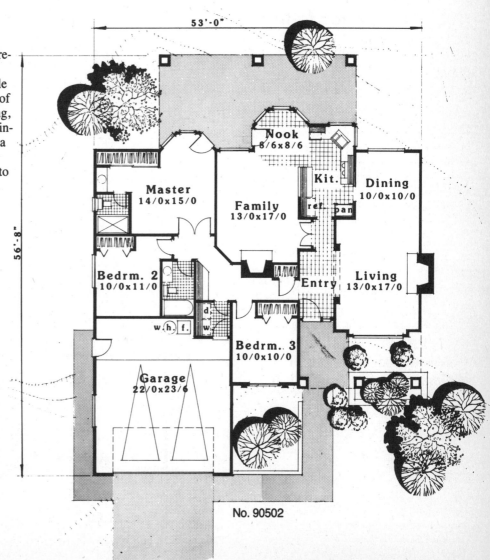

No. 90502

Storage Space Galore In Garage

No. 20065

This simple design's exterior features a large picture window and rock front. On the first floor from the foyer is a spacious living room with its own wood burning fireplace. The dining room lies in front of the living room and next to the kitchen. From the kitchen to the right is the breakfast room with access to a large outdoor wooden deck. A half bath and laundry facilities are other rooms on the first floor. On the second floor are three bedrooms. Two bedrooms share a full bath with its own skylight, while the master bedroom has its own private bath and walk-in closet. One final feature of this plan is the large amount of storage space available in the two-car garage.

First floor — 936 sq. ft.
Second floor — 777 sq. ft.
Garage/storage — 624 sq. ft.

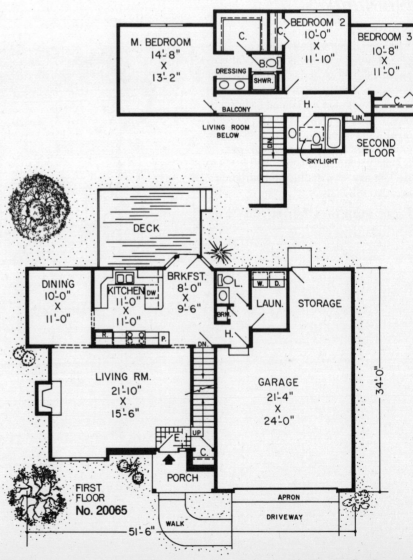

A Karl Kreeger Design

Open Plan Brightens Compact Dwelling

No. 90506

Open to the balcony above and the entry and dining room below, the vaulted great room is the highlight of this home. A central staircase winds its way up to three bedrooms, two baths, and a play room that doubles as storage. The master bedroom and breakfast nook feature bay windows that give both rooms a distinctive shape and cheerful atmosphere.

First floor — 996 sq. ft.
Second floor — 942 sq. ft.

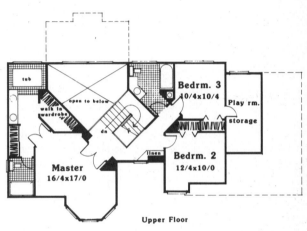

Upper Floor

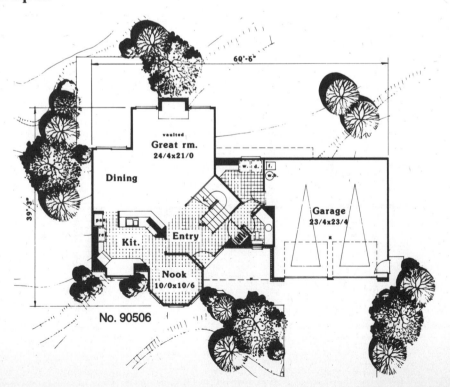

No. 90506

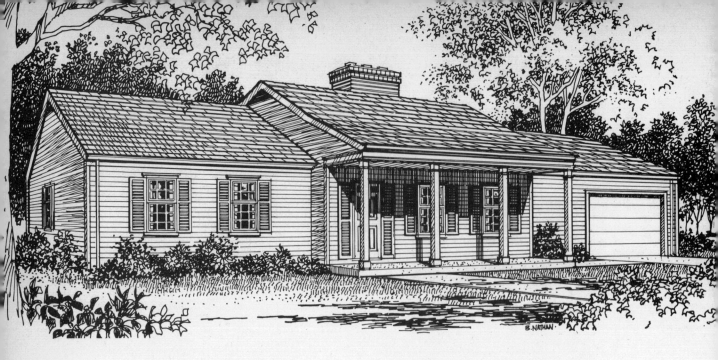

Early American Home for Today

No. 90605

This house reflects the charm and warmth that was prevalent in the early American home 200 years ago. The shuttered, double-hung windows, the moldings at the eaves, the large chimney, and the clapboard siding are elements that capture a colonial flavor. This is reflected in the interior, especially in the "Keeping Room", the early American family gathering place. Located to the rear of the living room, it's used for dining, cooking, and family fun. A counter-height fireplace, pegged plank flooring, beamed ceiling, and colonial-style kitchen cabinets continue the early American motif.

Total living area — 1,260 sq. ft. (optional slab construction available)

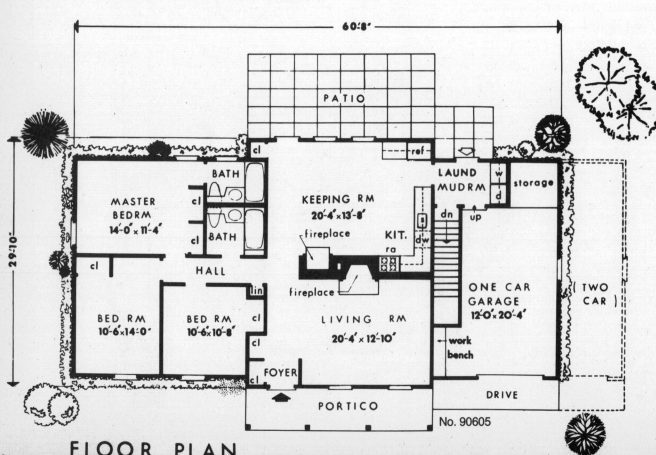

FLOOR PLAN

Roomy Ranch Design

No. 10594

This delightful ranch design utilizes space with great efficiency. Enter a tiled foyer and be greeted by an excellent floor plan designed to handle traffic. Off the foyer to the right, the great room has a sloping open beamed ceiling and a wood burning fireplace. A den/bedroom lies to the left of the foyer. Connected to the great room is the dining room and the kitchen. Sliding glass doors lead from the dining room out onto a large wooden deck. Other features in this plan include a laundry room and two other bedrooms that have their own full baths. A two-car garage is also added for convenience.

First — 1,565 sq. ft.
Basement — 1,576 sq. ft.
Garage — 430 sq. ft.

A Karl Kreeger Design

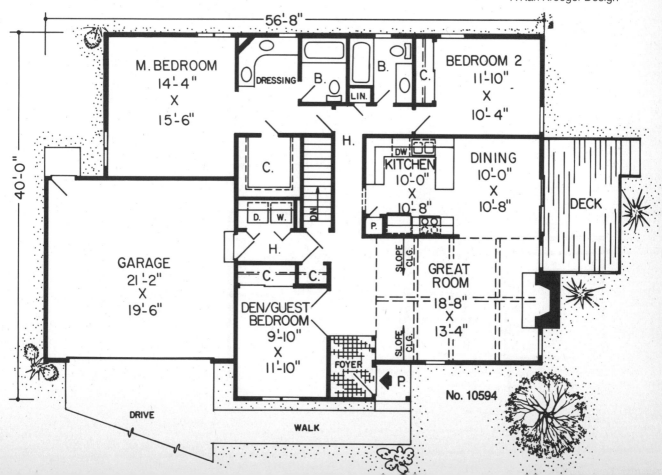

Covered Porch Offered in Farm-type Traditional

No. 20064

This pleasant traditional design has a farmhouse flavor exterior that incorporates a covered porch and features a circle wood louver on its garage, giving this design a feeling of sturdiness. Inside on the first level from the foyer and to the right is a formal dining room complete with a bay window and an elevated ceiling and a corner china cabinet. To the left of the foyer is the living room with a woodburning fireplace. The kitchen is connected to the breakfast room and there is a room for the laundry facilities. A half bath is also featured on the first floor. The second floor has three bedrooms. The master bedroom is on the second floor and has its own private bath and walk-in closet. The other two bedrooms share a full bath. A two-car garage is also added into this design.

First floor — 892 sq. ft.
Second floor — 836 sq. ft.
Basement — 892 sq. ft.
Garage — 491 sq. ft.

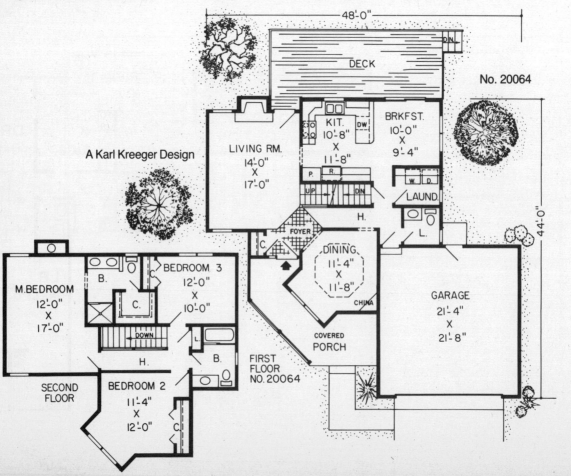

A Karl Kreeger Design

No. 20064

DECK

LIVING RM.
14'-0"
X
17'-0"

KIT.
10'-8"
X
11'-8"

BRKFST.
10'-0"
X
9'-4"

LAUND.

FOYER

UP
DN

H.

DINING
11'-4"
X
11'-8"

CHINA

COVERED PORCH

GARAGE
21'-4"
X
21'-8"

FIRST FLOOR
NO. 20064

M.BEDROOM
12'-0"
X
17'-0"

B.

C.

BEDROOM 3
12'-0"
X
10'-0"

DOWN

H.

B.

SECOND FLOOR

BEDROOM 2
11'-4"
X
12'-0"

48'-0"

44'-0"

Compact Design Provides for Family

No. 90300

This well organized design provides a separate half story for the three bedrooms plus two baths and plenty of closet space. The main floor employs the garage to buffer street noise. The front living room provides easy access to the rear dining room and the more informal areas of the home. Roomy closets are placed near the front entrance and at the family entrance through the garage. The half bath is located just off the kitchen which shares a counter with the adjacent family room. A fireplace plus sliding glass doors which open onto the rear deck make this a prime candidate for many cozy evenings.

Total area — 1,630 sq. ft.

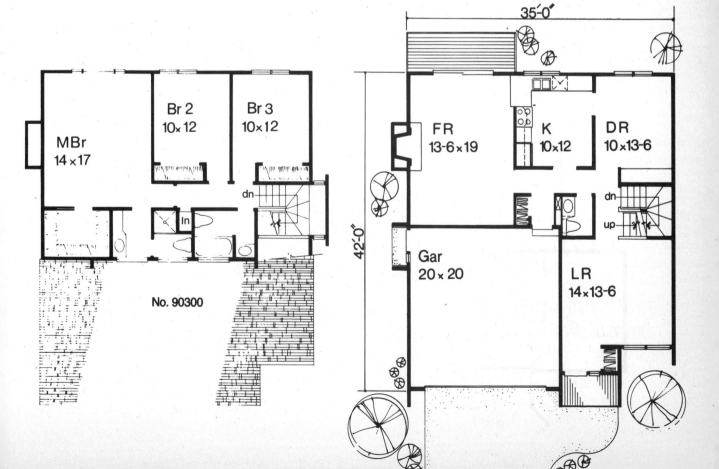

MBr 14 × 17

Br 2 10 × 12

Br 3 10 × 12

dn

No. 90300

FR 13-6 × 19

K 10 × 12

DR 10 × 13-6

dn

up

Gar 20 × 20

LR 14 × 13-6

35'-0"

42'-0"

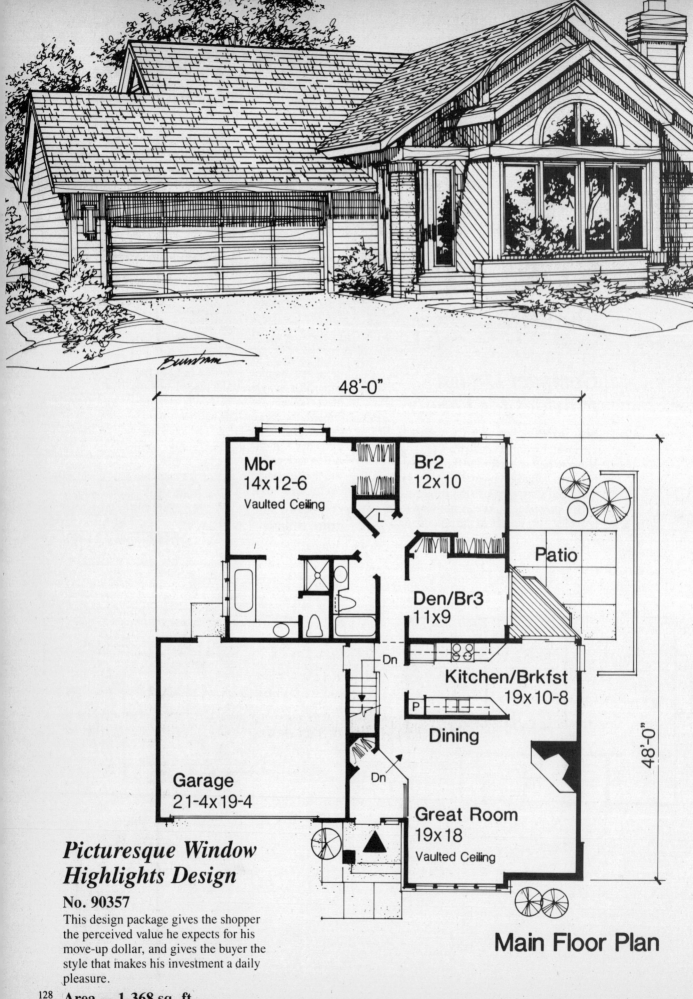

48'-0"

Mbr
14x12-6
Vaulted Ceiling

Br2
12x10

L

Patio

Den/Br3
11x9

Dn

Kitchen/Brkfst
19x10-8

P

Dining

Dn

Garage
21-4x19-4

Great Room
19x18
Vaulted Ceiling

48'-0"

Picturesque Window Highlights Design

No. 90357

This design package gives the shopper the perceived value he expects for his move-up dollar, and gives the buyer the style that makes his investment a daily pleasure.

128 **Area — 1,368 sq. ft.**

Main Floor Plan

Old-Fashioned Charm

No. 21124

An old fashioned, homespun flavor has been created using lattice work, horizontal and vertical placement of wood siding, and full-length front and rear porches with turned wood columns and wood railings. The floor plan features an open living room, dining room and kitchen. A master suite finishes the first level. An additional bedroom and full bath are located upstairs. Here, also, is found a large bonus room which could serve a variety of family needs. Or it can be deleted altogether by adding a second floor balcony overlooking the living room below and allowing the living room ceilings to spaciously rise two full stories. Wood floors throughout the design add a final bit of country to the plan. No materials list available for this plan.

First floor — 835 sq. ft.
Second floor — 817 sq. ft.

No materials list available

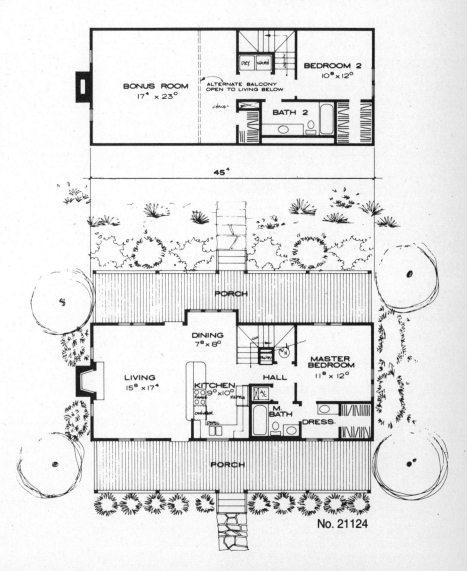

No. 21124

Timeless Character, Built-In Convenience

No. 90233

Imagine the possiblities in this sprawling, three-bedroom home, adaptable to any lifestyle. The family cook will love the warm, wide-open atmosphere of the efficient kitchen which adjoins a walk-in pantry and beamed family room. For the family that loves to entertain, the formal living and dining room off the foyer is just perfect. And, the first-floor master suite, complete with a private bath, adjoining study, and sliders to the terrace, means you won't have to climb the stairs at the end of the day. The central staircase leads to a cozy sitting room linking two spacious bedrooms and a full bath.

First floor — 1,500 sq. ft.
Second floor — 690 sq. ft.
Garage — 3-car

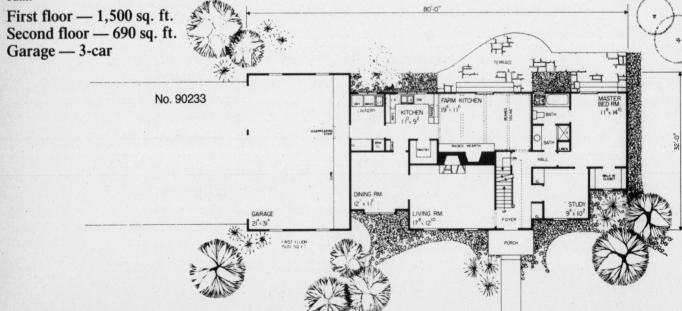

No. 90233

Impressive Use of Space

No. 90131

The great room is the focal point of this uniquely organized plan; its sloped ceiling rises two stories to the cozy second floor balcony. Also on the second floor is the master bedroom with its own balcony, double closets and roomy bath. The two first floor bedrooms are separated from the living areas by the stairway, a large bath and extra closets. The L-shaped kitchen is conveniently located between the dining area and the garage entrance. Additional kitchen features are the built-in grill and the sliding door to the patio. The laundry room is placed so that it can also serve as a mud room just inside the garage door.

First floor — 1,320 sq. ft.
Second floor — 444 sq. ft.

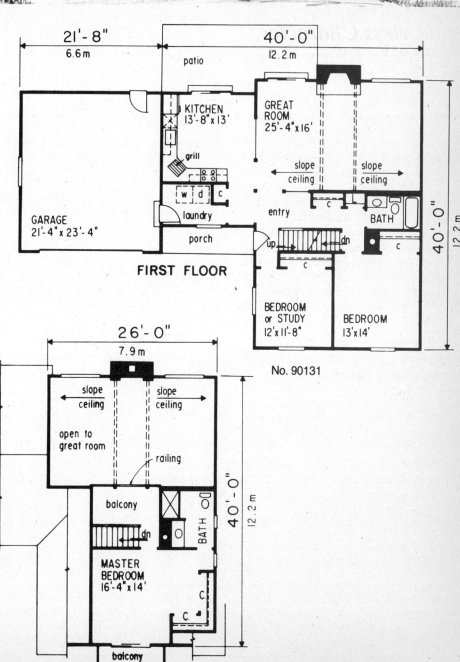

FIRST FLOOR

No. 90131

Stacked Windows Create Exciting Exterior

No. 20009

Here's a three-bedroom beauty that unites interior living spaces with the great outdoors. A generous supply of huge windows, easy access to a deck and patio off the dining and family rooms, and a plan that eliminates unnecessary walls all add up to a wide-open atmosphere you'll love. The kitchen features a convenient pass-through to the sunny breakfast bay. And, thanks to the open plan, the cook can enjoy the cozy warmth of the family room fireplace. Upstairs, the two rear bedrooms share a full bath with double vanities. The master suite, dominated by a stacked window arrangement, features cathedral ceilings and a private bath with a raised tub and walk-in shower.

First floor — 982 sq. ft.
Second floor — 815 sq. ft.
Basement — 978 sq. ft.

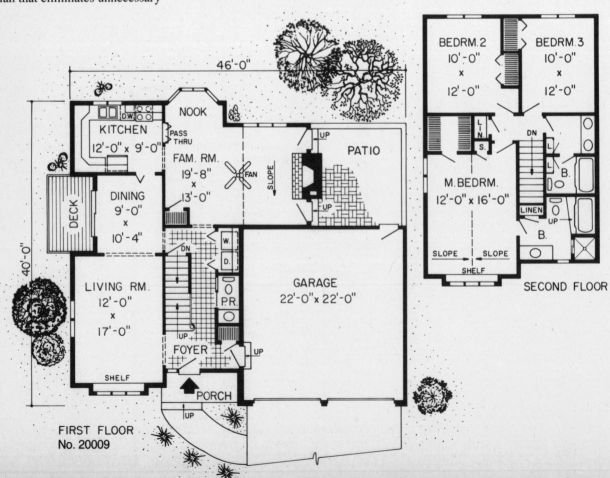

FIRST FLOOR
No. 20009

SECOND FLOOR

Compact Plan Allows For Gracious Living

No. 90158

A great room, accessible from the foyer, offers a cathedral ceiling with exposed beams, brick fireplace and access to the rear patio. The kitchen-breakfast area with center island and cathedral ceiling is accented by the round top window. The master bedroom has a full bath and walk-in closet. Two additional bedrooms and bath help make this an ideal plan for any growing family.

First floor—1,540 sq. ft.
Basement—1,540 sq. ft.

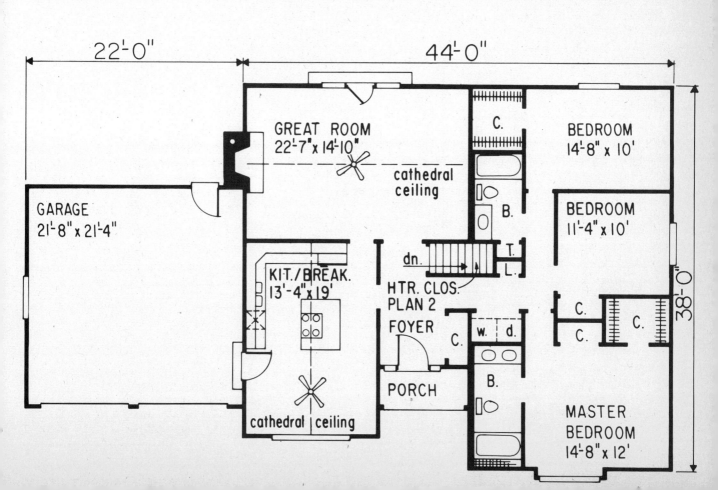

Classic Warmth

No. 10684

This compact traditional with clapboard exterior and inviting, sheltered entry boasts loads of features that make it a special home. Look at the built-in seat by the garage entry, the handy breakfast bar that separates the kitchen and family room, and the convenient powder room just off the foyer. Cathedral ceilings lend an airy quality to the living and dining rooms. A single step down keeps the two rooms separate without compromising the open feeling that's so enjoyable. Sliders lead from both dining and family rooms to the rear patio, making it an excellent location for an outdoor party.

Tucked upstairs, the three bedrooms include your own, private master suite.

First floor — 940 sq. ft.
Second floor — 720 sq. ft.
Walkout basement — 554 sq. ft.
Garage — 418 sq. ft.
Crawl space — 312 sq. ft.

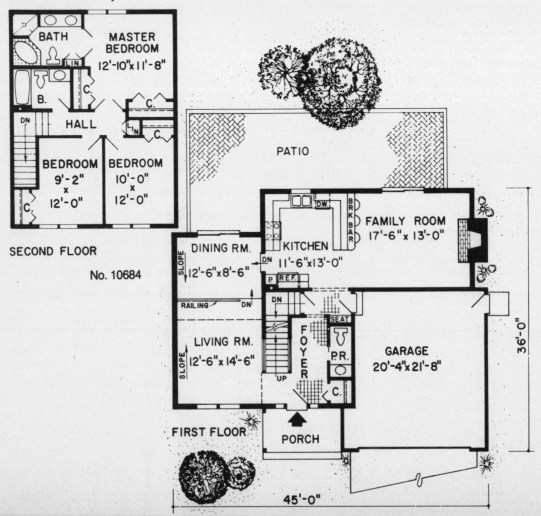

Perfect For Entertaining

No. 20050

As guests enter the two-story, tiled foyer, they are immediately welcomed by the expansive living room with its sloped ceiling and cheery fireplace. Lead them into the dining room and serve them from the adjacent kitchen. There's even room for more than one cook in this roomy kitchen which opens onto a covered deck for outdoor meals. The first floor master bedroom features a large, five-piece bath and double closets. Upstairs are two more bedrooms with roomy closets, an additional bath and room for storage in the attic.

First floor — 1,303 sq. ft.
Second floor — 596 sq. ft.
Basement — 1,303 sq. ft.
Garage — 460 sq. ft.

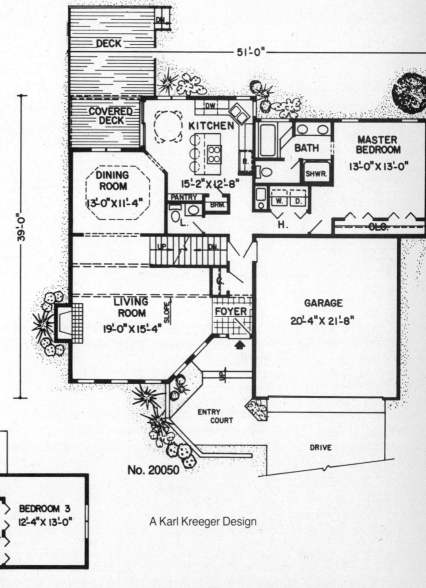

No. 20050

A Karl Kreeger Design

SECOND FLOOR
No. 20050

Build this on a Budget

No. 90544

Classic touches add exterior charm to this affordable, three-bedroom beauty. But inside, a wide-open plan keeps the walls from closing in. The covered entry opens to a formal living-dining room arrangement that's perfect for entertaining. And, whether you're dining in formal style or snacking in the breakfast nook in the fireplaced family room, the strategically located kitchen makes mealtime a breeze. Bedrooms are tucked upstairs for privacy. A full bath at the top of the stairs serves the front bedrooms, which feature angular entries that give each room an interesting shape. The master suite includes a bay window sitting area, two walls of closets, and a full bath with walk-in shower.

First floor — 882 sq. ft.
Second floor — 753 sq. ft.
Garage — 2-car

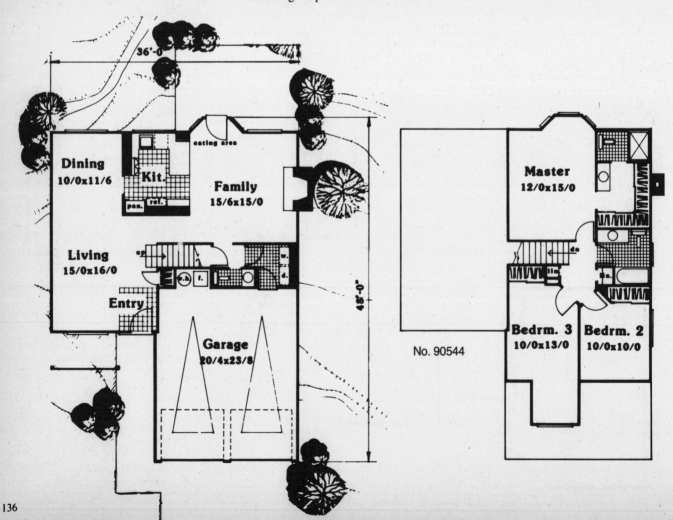

Design Incorporates Informal and Formal

No. 90317

The main level of this two-story home is divided into formal and informal living areas by the central placement of the staircase and the kitchen. The two-story living room and the dining room with its unique bump-out window are located to one side of the home. On the other side are the family room with its inviting fireplace and the breakfast room which has sliding glass doors onto the deck. Four bedrooms comprise the second floor. The expansive master bedroom features a five-piece bath and two walk-in closets.

Main level — 1,413 sq. ft.
Upper level — 1,245 sq. ft.
Basement — 1,413 sq. ft.
Garage — 689 sq. ft.

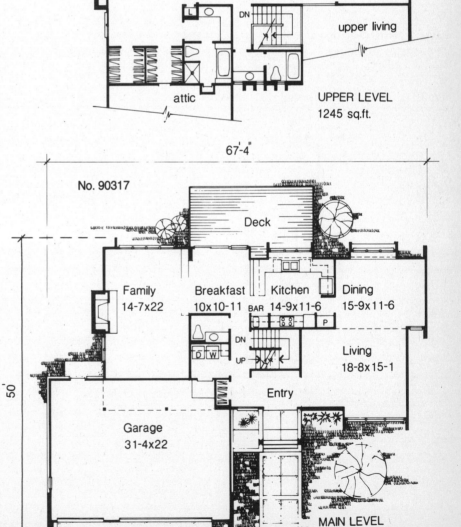

MBr. 13x20-7
Br. 4 10x10
Br. 3 12-7x10
Br. 2 10-5x13-6
DN
upper living
attic
UPPER LEVEL
1245 sq.ft.

No. 90317
67'-4"
Deck
Family 14-7x22
Breakfast 10x10-11
BAR
Kitchen 14-9x11-6
Dining 15-9x11-6
P
DN
D W
UP
Living 18-8x15-1
Entry
50'
Garage 31-4x22
MAIN LEVEL

Country Classic Full of Character

No. 90397

Towering gables softened by gentle arches add old-fashioned charm to this tidy, three-bedroom traditional. But, look at the updated interior. Corner transom windows create a sunny atmosphere throughout the open plan. A fireplace divides the vaulted living room and dining room, contributing to the spacious, yet warm feeling in this inviting home. Any cook would envy the efficient layout of the country kitchen, with its corner sink overlooking the deck and family sitting area. And, even your plants will enjoy the greenhouse atmosphere of the vaulted master suite, which features a double-vanitied bath and walk-in closet. Another full bath serves the children's rooms.

First floor — 834 sq. ft.
Second floor — 722 sq. ft.
Garage — 2-car

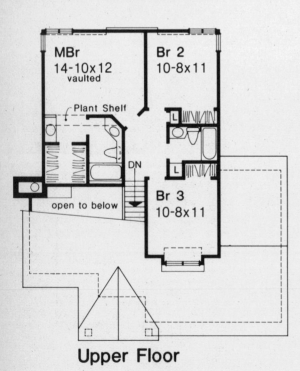

Upper Floor

MBr 14-10x12 vaulted
Br 2 10-8x11
Plant Shelf
open to below
DN
Br 3 10-8x11

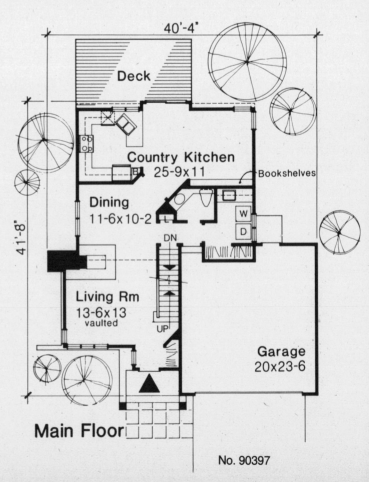

Main Floor

No. 90397

40'-4"
41'-8"
Deck
Country Kitchen 25-9x11
Bookshelves
Dining 11-6x10-2
W D
DN
Living Rm 13-6x13 vaulted
UP
Garage 20x23-6

Designed for Informal Life Style

No. 90325

You'll find daily living relaxed and comfortable in this stylish plan. Both the great room and the kitchen/dining room of this home are accented by vaulted ceilings. In addition to having a conveniently arranged L-shaped food preparation center, the dining area overlooks the deck through sliding glass doors. The great room incorporates all adjacent floor space and is highlighted by the corner placement of the fireplace. Two bedrooms are secluded from the living areas and feature individual access to the full bath. The master bedroom also includes a separate vanity in the dressing area.

Main floor — 988 sq. ft.
Basement — 988 sq. ft.
Garage — 400 sq. ft.

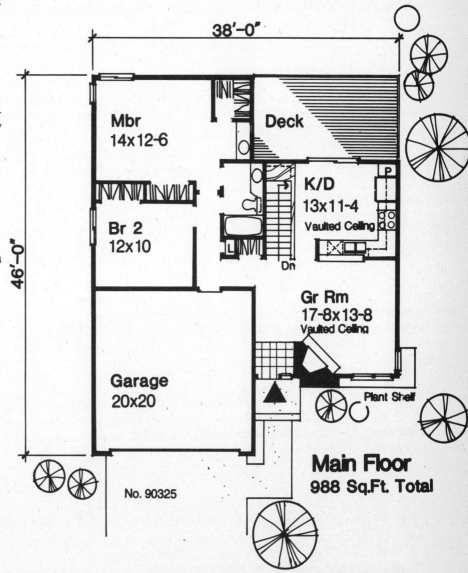

38'-0"

46'-0"

Mbr
14x12-6

Deck

Br 2
12x10

K/D
13x11-4
Vaulted Ceiling

Dn

Gr Rm
17-8x13-8
Vaulted Ceiling

Garage
20x20

Plant Shelf

No. 90325

Main Floor
988 Sq.Ft. Total

Build This One-Level Home on a Budget

No. 90235

Here's an L-shaped ranch that will house your family in style without breaking your building budget. Stand in the central entry and enjoy the view of the large living room, a massive fireplace and the rear terrace beyond the sliding glass doors. Eat in the rear-facing privacy of the formal dining room, or in the spacious country kitchen. You'll appreciate the nearby garage entry when your arms are full of groceries. Three bedrooms and two full baths off the entry include the master suite with private terrace access.

Main living area — 1,267 sq. ft.
Garage — 2-car

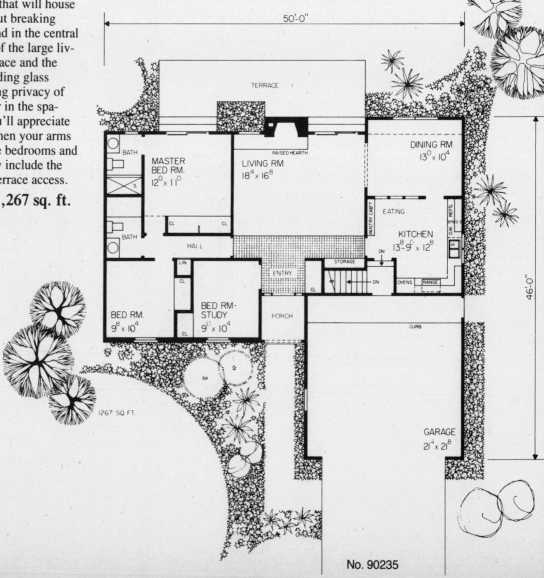

No. 90235

Open Floor Plan Enhanced by Sloped Ceilings

No. 90125

A step down from the tiled entrance area, guests may overlook an expansive living area composed of the great room and the dining room. Warmed by a fireplace and further enhanced by sliding doors opening onto the patio, this welcoming area is easily served by the L-shaped kitchen which shares a snack bar with the dining room. The three bedrooms are separated from the living areas by the careful placement of the bathrooms and the laundry. The master bedroom features two closets, including a walk-in, plus a private bath.

Living area — 1,440 sq. ft.

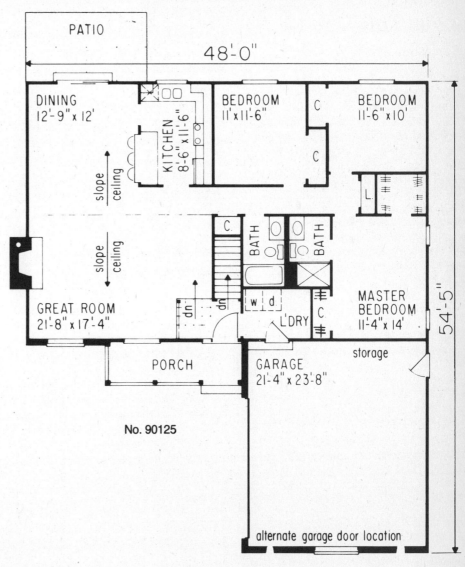

PATIO

48'-0"

54'-5"

DINING
12'-9" x 12'

KITCHEN
8'-6" x 11'-6"

BEDROOM
11' x 11'-6"

C

BEDROOM
11'-6" x 10'

C

slope ceiling

slope ceiling

L

BATH

BATH

C.

w d

MASTER
BEDROOM
11'-4" x 14'

GREAT ROOM
21'-8" x 17'-4"

dn   dn

L'DRY

C

storage

PORCH

GARAGE
21'-4" x 23'-8"

No. 90125

alternate garage door location

Compact Two-Story Design Ideal For Small Lot

No. 10517

Extra space is provided by the intricate angles incorporated into this design. The living room has a sloped ceiling and tiled hearth. The angular kitchen has direct access to the rear deck. A two-story foyer leads to the second floor which has two bedrooms, a bath, and individual dressing rooms. The master suite has a walk-in closet and complete bath.

First floor — 1,171 sq. ft.
Second floor — 561 sq. ft.
Basement — 1,171 sq. ft.
Garage — 484 sq. ft.

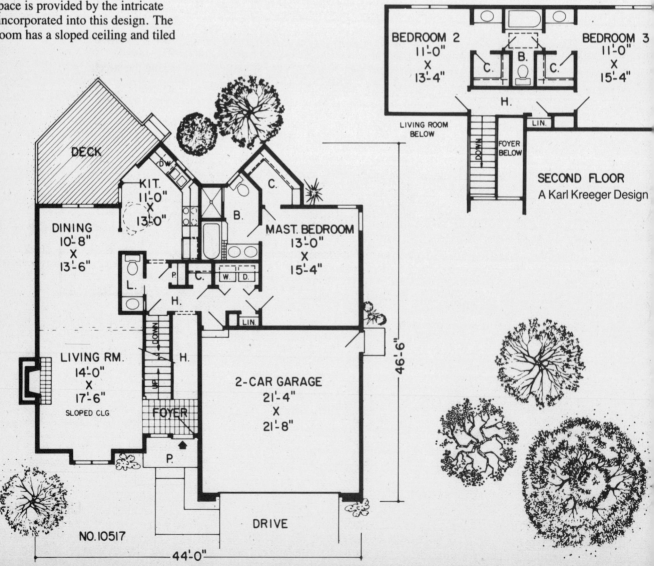

BEDROOM 2
11'-0"
X
13'-4"

BEDROOM 3
11'-0"
X
15'-4"

B.

H.

LIN.

LIVING ROOM BELOW

FOYER BELOW

DOWN

SECOND FLOOR
A Karl Kreeger Design

DECK

KIT.
11'-0"
X
13'-0"

DINING
10'-8"
X
13'-6"

B.

C.

MAST. BEDROOM
13'-0"
X
15'-4"

L.

P.

C.

W.

D.

H.

LIN.

LIVING RM.
14'-0"
X
17'-6"
SLOPED CLG

DOWN

H.

FOYER

P.

2-CAR GARAGE
21'-4"
X
21'-8"

46'-6"

DRIVE

NO. 10517

44'-0"

A Modern Home with a Traditional Face

No. 90399

Here's a masterpiece of timeless design that's been updated for today's busy family. Classic elements, from the covered front porch to the central staircase and the cozy family room fireplace, add traditional warmth to this compact home. But, the addition of abundant windows and eliminating unnecessary walls achieves a spacious feeling throughout active areas. You'll appreciate the strategic kitchen location, between breakfast and formal dining rooms, and the rear deck that allows you to keep your eyes on the kids while you're busy in the kitchen. Three bedrooms and two full baths upstairs include the roomy master suite, which features a half-round, vaulted window overlooking the street.

First floor — 984 sq. ft.
Second floor — 744 sq. ft.

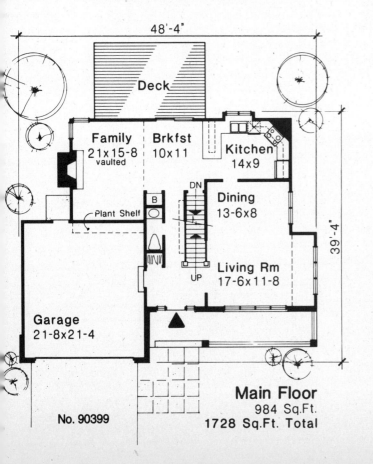

Main Floor
984 Sq.Ft.
1728 Sq.Ft. Total

No. 90399

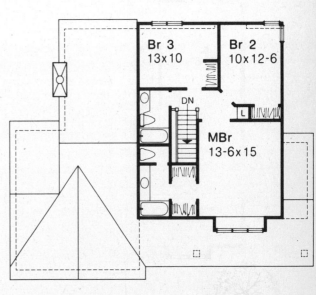

Upper Floor
744 Sq.Ft.

Vaulted Views

No. 91416

Multiple peaks and half-round windows hint at the dramatic interior of this exciting, three-bedroom contemporary. Inside the foyer, treat yourself to a view of an expansive, two-story great room and full-length deck beyond the atrium doors. The great room, dining room, and kitchen with rangetop island flow together for an outdoor feeling accentuated by lots of glass. Corner windows and a hot tub give the first-floor master suite the same, magnificent ambience. If you prefer to relax inside, use the garden tub or step-in shower just past the his-and-hers walk-in closets. A balcony at the top of the stairs overlooks the fire-placed great room below, leading to two more bedrooms with an adjoining full bath.

First floor — 1,440 sq. ft.
Second floor — 640 sq. ft.
Bonus room — 220 sq. ft.
Garage — 2-car

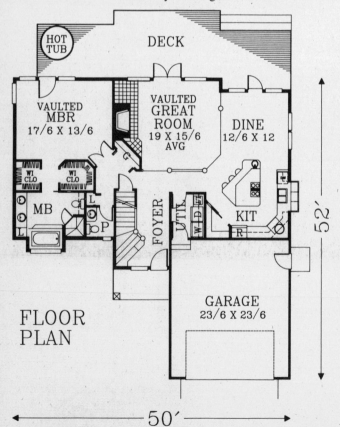

FLOOR PLAN

No. 91416

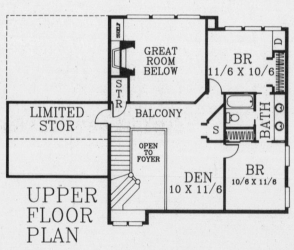

UPPER FLOOR PLAN

Eating Options Offered

No. 10421

The kitchen's location next to the nook and dining room, and only steps away from the covered patio, offers numerous options for both formal and informal dining. The kitchen is well-planned to save steps during food preparation, yet roomy enough for someone who likes to spread out. The dining area, which can be shut off from the kitchen by way of wood folding doors, is sunken 6 inches and lit with natural light from six 6 ft. windows. Glass variations across the front exterior also include arched gameroom windows, three arched windows in the master suite which form a box type bay, three 7'6" living room leaded windows and leaded skylight and transom at entry.

First floor — 1,605 sq. ft.
Second floor — 732 sq. ft.
Garage — 525 sq. ft.
Patio — 395 sq. ft.

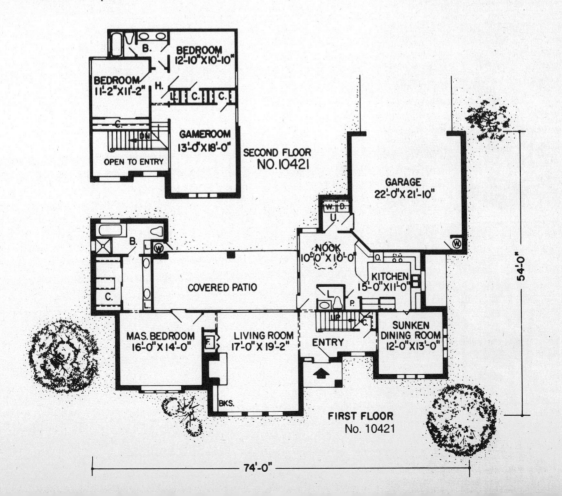

SECOND FLOOR
NO. 10421

BEDROOM
12'-10" X 10'-10"

BEDROOM
11'-2" X 11'-2"

GAMEROOM
13'-0" X 18'-0"

OPEN TO ENTRY

GARAGE
22'-0" X 21'-10"

NOOK
10'-0" X 10'-0"

KITCHEN
15'-0" X 11'-0"

COVERED PATIO

MAS. BEDROOM
16'-0" X 14'-0"

LIVING ROOM
17'-0" X 19'-2"

ENTRY

SUNKEN
DINING ROOM
12'-0" X 13'-0"

BKS.

54'-0"

74'-0"

FIRST FLOOR
No. 10421

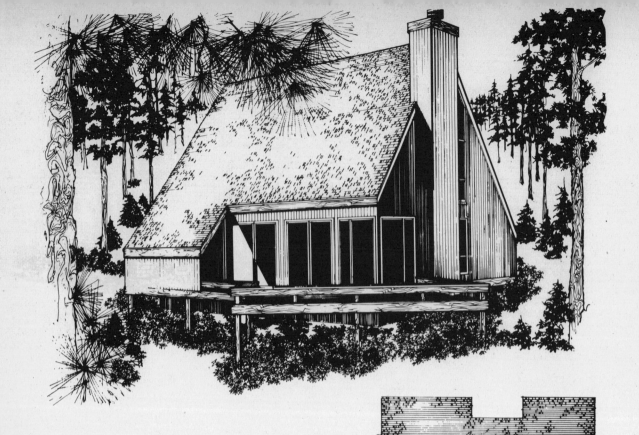

Modified A-frame At Home Anywhere

No. 90309

Comfortable living in this compact plan is equally at home in suburbia or at a resort. The main floor includes a combined living room/dining room whose ceiling reaches to the second floor loft. This living area is further enhanced by its view of the angled deck through corner windows and two sliding glass doors, plus the fireplace with its large hearth. Located at one end of the rear deck is a roomy outdoor storage cabinet. The galley-style kitchen is conveniently arranged and is located near both the front entrance and the laundry area for convenience. Completing the main floor are a bedroom and a full bath. In addition to the loft on the second floor, there are an optional bedroom and a half bath.

Main floor-735 sq. ft.
Upper floor-304 sq. ft.

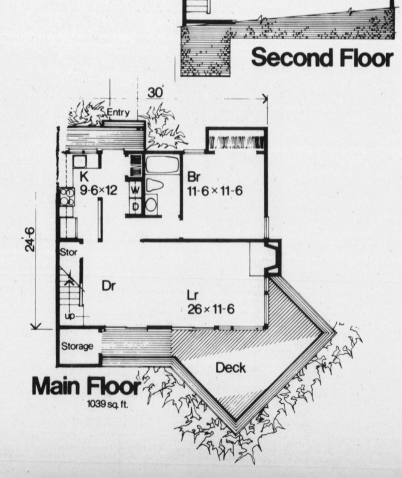

146

Compact Home Has Open Design

No. 10455

The airlock entry saves energy and opens onto the tiled foyer which extends inward toward the adjacent dining and living rooms. The living room has a window wall which overlooks the lawn, a fireplace with hearth, built-in bookcases, a wet bar and direct access to the patio. The dining room has direct access to the step-saver kitchen with its plentiful storage and convenient peninsula. Along the opposite side of the house are the three bedrooms. Individual dressing areas within the master suite include separate vanities and walk-in closets.

First floor — 1,643 sq. ft.
Garage — 500 sq. ft.

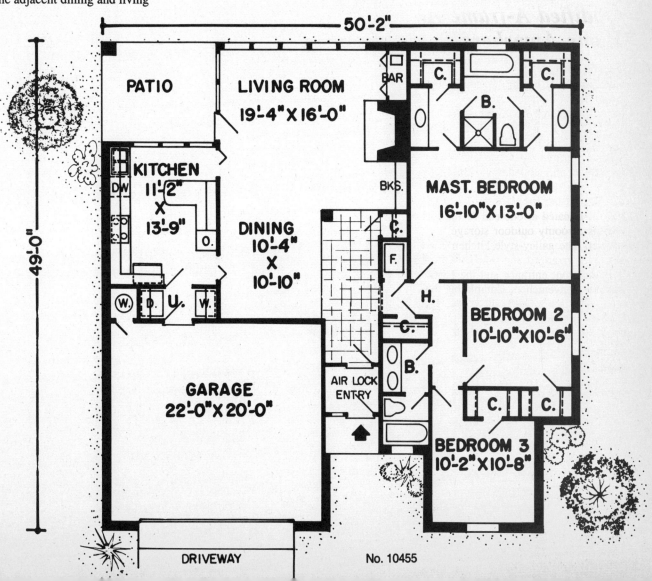

No. 10455

Master Suite Crowns Plan

No. 10394

The master bedroom suite occupies the entire second level of this passive solar design. The living room rises two stories in the front, as does the foyer, and can be opened to the master suite to aid in air circulation. Skylights in the sloping ceil- ings of the kitchen and master bath give abundant light to these areas. Angled walls, both inside and out, lend a unique appeal. An air lock entry, 2X6 exterior studs, 6-inch concrete floor, and gener- ous use of insulation help make this an energy efficient design.

First floor — 1,306 sq. ft.
Second floor — 472 sq. ft.
Garage — 576 sq. ft.

20'-2"

32'-10"

DRESSING AREA

C.   C.

SITTING AREA

MASTER BEDROOM SUITE
19'-2"X15'-7"

OPEN TO ENTRY

OPEN TO LIVING ROOM

SECOND FLOOR

68'-0"

UP

PATIO

DECK

S.

UTIL.

D. W.

F.

P.

S.

BRM

HW

S.

B.

C.

BEDROOM
12'-10"X11'-4"

DOUBLE GARAGE
23'-8" X 23'-4"

KITCHEN
11'-6"X
11'-8"

L.

C.

PLANTER

HALL

C.

34'-10"

DINING ROOM
11'-6"X10'-0"

AIR-LOCK ENTRY

LIVING ROOM
13'-0"X20'-3"

BEDROOM
11'-6"X13'-0"

WOOD STOVE

DRIVEWAY

W.

PORCH

NO. 10394

FIRST FLOOR

Tasteful Elegance
Aim of Design

No. 22020
With an exterior that expresses French Provincial charm, this single level design emphasizes elegance and offers a semi-circular dining area overlooking the patio. To pamper parents, the master bedroom annexes a long dressing area and private bath, while another bath serves the second and third bedrooms. A wood-burning fireplace furnishes the family room.

House proper — 1,772 sq. ft.
Garage — 469 sq. ft.

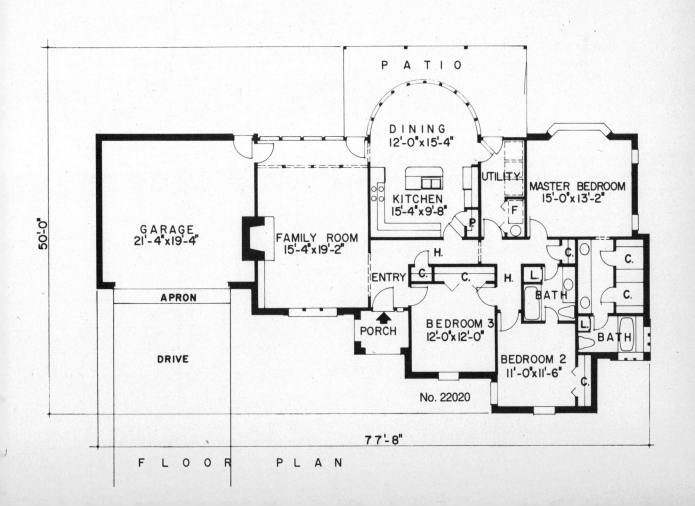

PATIO

DINING
12'-0"x15'-4"

UTILITY

MASTER BEDROOM
15'-0"x13'-2"

KITCHEN
15'-4"x9'-8"

GARAGE
21'-4"x19'-4"

FAMILY ROOM
15'-4"x19'-2"

H.

C.

C.

ENTRY

C. C.

H.

L.

BATH

C.

C.

APRON

PORCH

BEDROOM 3
12'-0"x12'-0"

L.

BATH

DRIVE

BEDROOM 2
11'-0"x11'-6"

C.

No. 22020

50'-0"

77'-8"

F L O O R   P L A N

One-Level Living is a Breeze

No. 10656

Zoned for privacy and convenience, this contemporary ranch is a perfect home for people who like to entertain. The central foyer divides quiet and active areas. Sound deadening closets and a full bath with double vanities keep the noise to a minimum in the bedroom wing. The deck off the master suite is a nice, private retreat for sunbathing or stargazing. Look at the recessed ceilings and bay windows in the dining room off the foyer. What a beautiful room for a candlelit dinner. Living areas at the rear of the house surround a brick patio so guests can enjoy the outdoors in nice weather. And, the open plan of the kitchen, nook, and vaulted great room keep traffic flowing smoothly, even when there's a crowd.

First floor — 1,899 sq. ft.
Basement — 1,890 sq. ft.
Garage — 530 sq. ft.

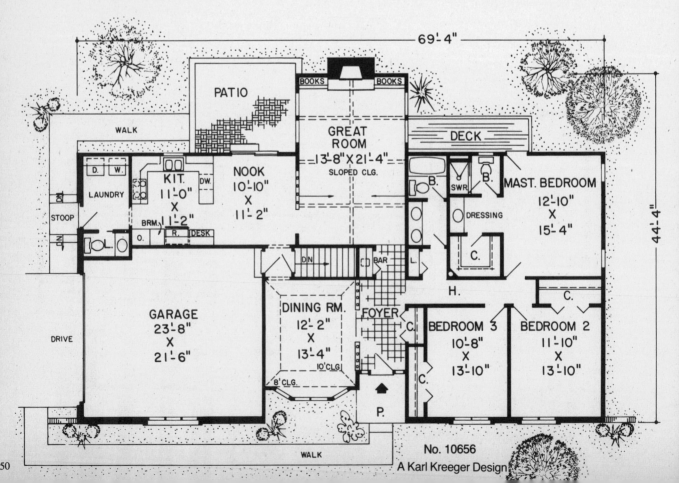

No. 10656
A Karl Kreeger Design

Sun Space Warms To Entertaining

No. 10495

Tile is used to soak up solar heat in the sun space and also to add a tailored accent to the total home arrangement. Leading from the air-lock entry torward the living room spaces of this marvelous home, the tile separates the activity areas from the sleeping quarters. With two bedrooms on the second story, the lower area includes the master bedroom suite with its divided bath and walk-in closet. The utilitarian areas of the home are also enhanced by direct access to the sun space plus a space-stretching central island.

First floor — 1,691 sq. ft.
Second floor — 512 sq. ft.
Garage — 484 sq. ft.
Sun space — 108 sq. ft.
Basement — 1,691 sq. ft.

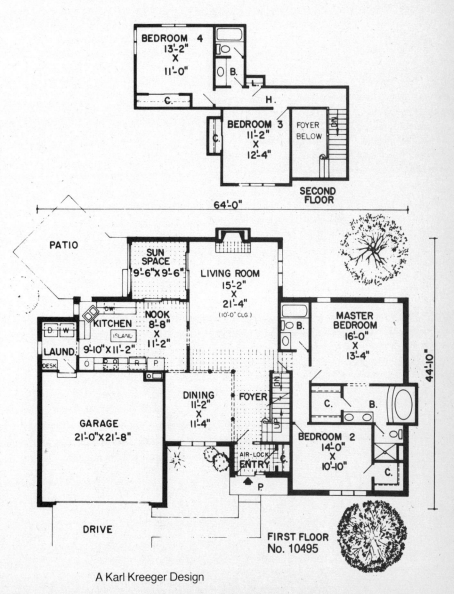

A Karl Kreeger Design

Rustic Exterior; Complete Home

No. 10140

Although rustic in appearance, the interior of this cabin is quiet, modern and comfortable. Small in overall size, it still contains three bedrooms and two baths in addition to a large, two-story living room with exposed beams. As a hunting-fishing lodge or mountain retreat, this compares well.

First floor — 1,008 sq. ft.
Second floor — 281 sq. ft.
Basement — 1,008 sq. ft.

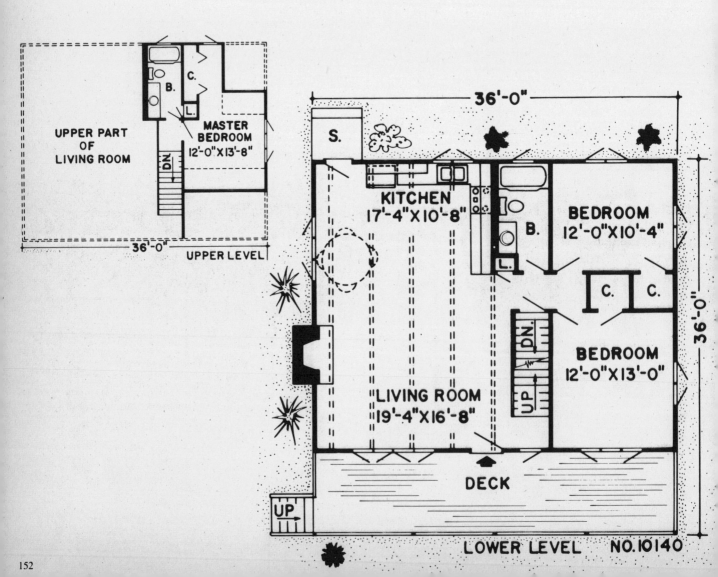

UPPER PART OF LIVING ROOM

B.

C.

L.

DN.

MASTER BEDROOM
12'-0" X 13'-8"

36'-0" UPPER LEVEL

36'-0"

S.

KITCHEN
17'-4" X 10'-8"

B.

L.

BEDROOM
12'-0" X 10'-4"

C. C.

BEDROOM
12'-0" X 13'-0"

DN.

UP

LIVING ROOM
19'-4" X 16'-8"

36'-0"

DECK

UP

LOWER LEVEL   NO. 10140

Open Plan Features Great Room and Exterior Options

No. 90328

With a skylight and a vaulted ceiling, the great room will welcome family and guests alike. This inviting room also includes a fireplace, sliding door access to the deck and a wet bar. The roomy eat-in kitchen features an efficient U-shaped work area and lots of windows in the dining area. The three bedrooms and two full baths incorporate unusual angled entries so as to make the most of every foot of floor space. The master bedroom combines its bath and dressing area. The third bedroom would make a cozy den or a handy room for guests.

Main floor — 1,400 sq. ft.
Basement — 1,350 sq. ft.
Garage — 374 sq. ft.

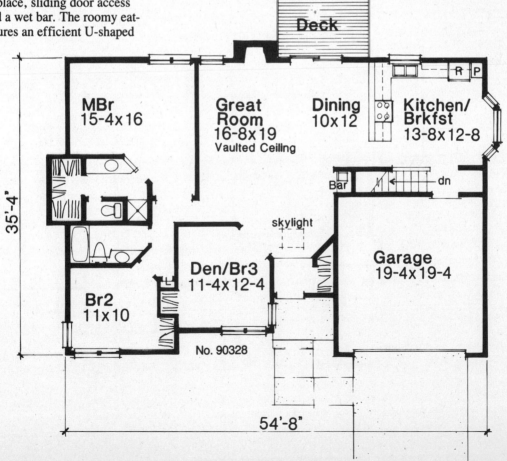

Compact and Appealing

No. 20075

Here's an L-shaped country charmer with a porch that demands a rocking chair or two. You'll appreciate the convenient one-level design that separates active and sleeping areas. Right off the foyer, the formal dining and living rooms have a wide-open feeling, thanks to extra wide doorways and a recessed ceiling. The kitchen is centrally located for maximum convenience. For informal family meals, you'll delight in the sunny breakfast nook that links the fireplaced living room and outdoor deck. Enjoy those quiet hours in the three bedrooms separated from family living spaces. With its own double-sink full bath and walk-in closet, the master suite will be your favorite retreat.

First floor — 1,682 sq. ft.
Basement — 1,682 sq. ft.
Garage — 484 sq. ft.

A Karl Kreeger Design

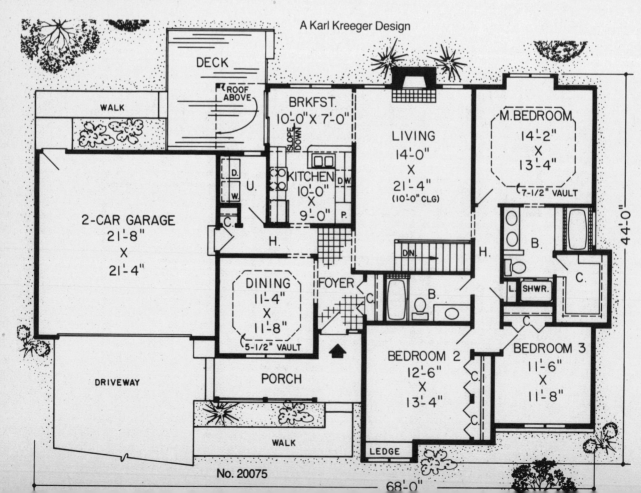

Glass Brings The Outdoors In

No. 9594

Adaptability is the outstanding characteristic of this modern two bedroom home. Imagine a folding partition wall that can enclose part of the expansive dining room to form a guest room or den. When the partitions are not in use, the living room and dining room, separated from the terrace only by sliding glass doors, offer an immense area for entertaining or relaxing. The kitchen is distinguished by an exposed brick wall which encloses the built-in oven.

First floor — 1,140 sq. ft.
Basement — 1,140 sq. ft.
Garage — 462 sq. ft.

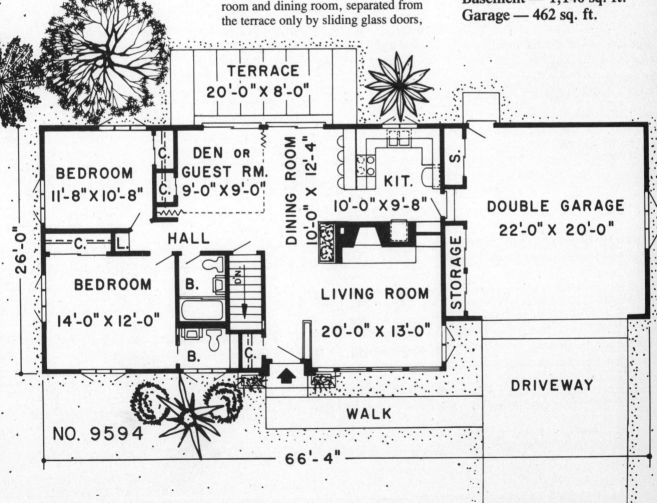

Good Things Come in Small Packages

No. 90264

With its compact plan and bonus space over the garage, this adaptable, Colonial gem can be built today, and grow along with your family later. The formal facade, with its balanced windows and front door, is a traditional introduction to the appealing interior. The entry opens to a fireplaced living room, which flows into the dining room overlooking the backyard. And, the well-appointed kitchen is spacious enough for informal family suppers. The first-floor powder room, and two full baths serving the three bedrooms upstairs, handle the early morning rush with ease. Imagine the cozy atmosphere you'll enjoy in the future office, study, or extra bedroom over the garage.

First floor — 624 sq. ft.
Second floor — 624 sq. ft.
Garage — 2-car

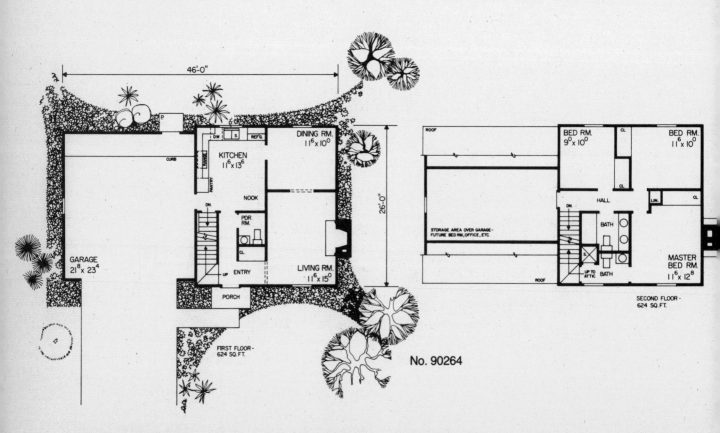

No. 90264

Traditional Ranch Design

No. 90146

This ranch design combines brick veneer with vertical siding exposing a traditional exterior whose interior contains three bedrooms and two full baths. Additionally, the floor plan is very open and unobstructed by wall partitions. The kitchen is very large and has its own eating area. The master bedroom is spacious and has a private bath. The utility room includes laundry facilities.

Main living area — 1,500 sq. ft.

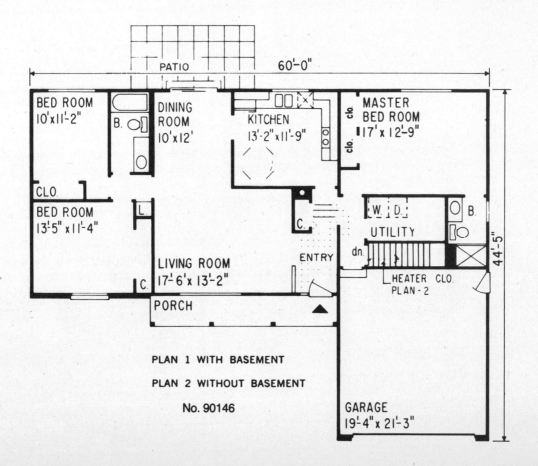

PATIO   60'-0"

BED ROOM 10'x11'-2"   B.   DINING ROOM 10'x12'   KITCHEN 13'-2"x11'-9"   clo. clo.   MASTER BED ROOM 17'x12'-9"

CLO.

BED ROOM 13'-5"x11'-4"   L.   W. D.   B.   UTILITY

C.   LIVING ROOM 17'-6'x13'-2"   ENTRY   dn.   44'-5"

C.   HEATER CLO. PLAN-2

PORCH

PLAN 1 WITH BASEMENT

PLAN 2 WITHOUT BASEMENT

No. 90146

GARAGE 19'-4"x21'-3"

Detailed Ranch Design

No. 90360

Stylish houses, to suit the higher design expectations of the sophisticated first-time and move-up buyers, need to present a lot of visible values. Starting with the very modern exterior look of this home with its arcaded living room sash, through its interior vaulted spaces and interesting master bedroom suite, this house says "buy me". Foundation off-sets are kept to the front where they count for character; simple main roof frames over main house body and master bedroom are cantilevered. Note, too, the easy option of eliminating the third bedroom closet and opening this room to the kitchen as a family room plus two bedroom home.

Main level — 1,283 sq. ft.

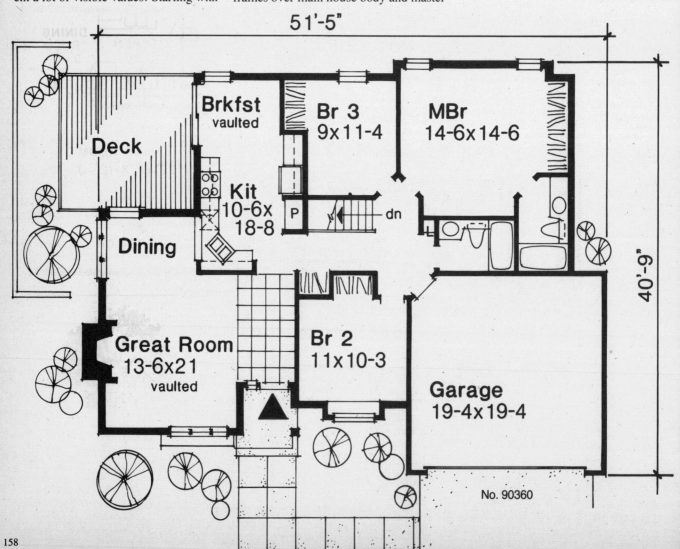

Rustic Comfort and Charm

No. 9076

Vacation in rustic comfort. Natural wood siding and a stone chimney highlight the charm of this plan. Sit back on the roomy front porch and enjoy old fashioned peace and quiet. And inside, where the fireplace lights the living and dining rooms, enjoy modern conveniences like the efficient kitchen, roomy closets, and enough bathrooms for a houseful of guests. The main floor of the house is designed compactly so that a retired couple faces a minimum of upkeep, yet the additional bedrooms offer plenty of room for company. Notice that the bedrooms close off tightly to conserve heating bills. This home can be built on a slab foundation.

First floor — 1,140 sq. ft.
Basement — 1,140 sq. ft.

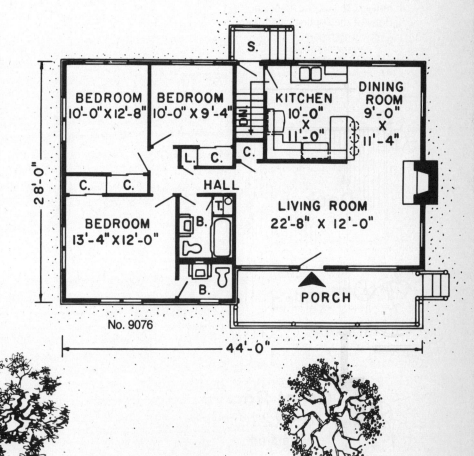

BEDROOM 10'-0" X 12'-8"
BEDROOM 10'-0" X 9'-4"
KITCHEN 10'-0" X 11'-0"
DINING ROOM 9'-0" X 11'-4"
S.
DN.
L. C.
C.
C. C.
HALL
BEDROOM 13'-4" X 12'-0"
T.
B.
LIVING ROOM 22'-8" X 12'-0"
B.
PORCH
28'-0"
44'-0"
No. 9076

Fireplace In Living and Family Room

No. 9263

This beautiful ranch design features an extra large living room with plenty of formal dining space at the opposite end. Large wood burning fireplaces are found in both the living and family rooms. A mud room, located off the kitchen, features a laundry area, half bath, and storage closet. The charming master bedroom has a full bath and plenty of closet space.

First floor — 1,878 sq. ft.
Garage — 538 sq. ft.

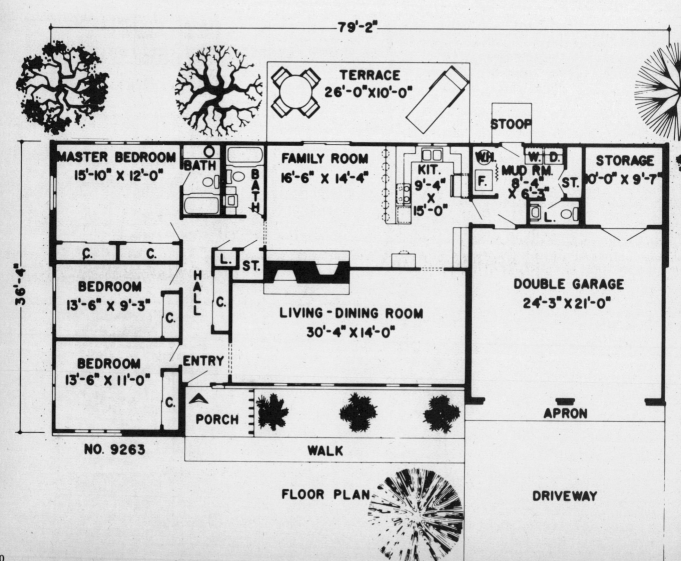

79'-2"

36'-4"

TERRACE 26'-0" X 10'-0"

STOOP

MASTER BEDROOM 15'-10" X 12'-0"

BATH

BATH

FAMILY ROOM 16'-6" X 14'-4"

KIT. 9'-4" X 15'-0"

W.H.

F.

MUD RM. 8'-4" X 6'-3"

W. D.

ST.

L.

STORAGE 10'-0" X 9'-7"

C.   C.

BEDROOM 13'-6" X 9'-3"

C.

HALL

L.   ST.

C.

DOUBLE GARAGE 24'-3" X 21'-0"

LIVING - DINING ROOM 30'-4" X 14'-0"

BEDROOM 13'-6" X 11'-0"

C.

ENTRY

PORCH

NO. 9263

WALK

APRON

FLOOR PLAN

DRIVEWAY

Three Bedroom Design Features Sloped Ceilings, Octagonal Rooms

No. 10505

The luxurious master suite of this uniquely designed, three bedroom home is secluded on an upper floor. It is linked to the stairway by a balcony which overlooks the first floor family room and central hall. Additionally it features a full wall of double closets, a sloped ceiling and a private fireplace. The octagonal, five-piece bath also features a sloped ceiling. The octagonal treatment is carried out in the first floor nook which adjoins the kitchen and in the arrangement of the casement windows in the living room. The family room boasts a corner fireplace and has its own sloped ceiling. Two additional bedrooms, each with a large closet, a four-piece bath, and a conveniently located laundry room complete this unusual and inviting home.

First floor — 1,704 sq. ft.
Second floor — 561 sq. ft.
Garage — 439 sq. ft.

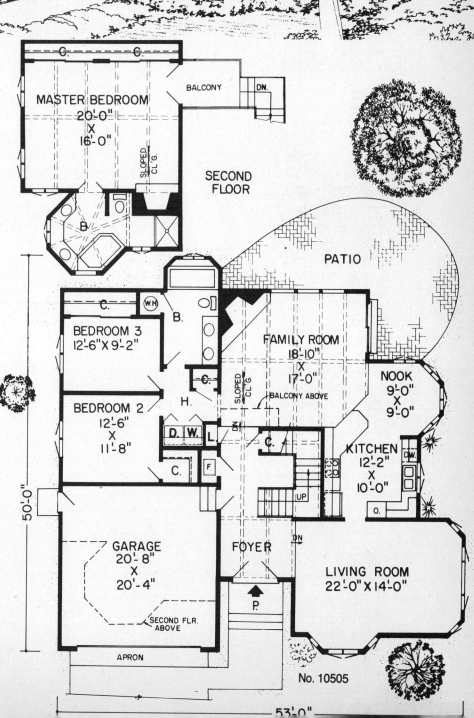

Terrace Doubles Outdoor Living Space

No. 90683

Here's a charming ranch that is loaded with amenities for today's busy family. A covered porch lends a welcoming touch to this compact, yet spacious home adorned with a wood and stone exterior.

A heat circulating fireplace makes the living room a comfortable, cozy place for relaxing. Family areas enjoy an airy greenhouse atmosphere, with three skylights piercing the high, sloping ceilings of this wide-open space. A glass wall and sliders to the terrace add to the outdoor feeling. You'll appreciate the pass-over convenience of the side-by-side kitchen

and dining room. And, you'll love the private master suite at the far end of the bedroom wing, with its bay window seat and private bath.

Main living area — 1,498 sq. ft.
Mudroom-laundry — 69 sq. ft.
Basement — 1,413 sq. ft.
Garage — 490 sq. ft.

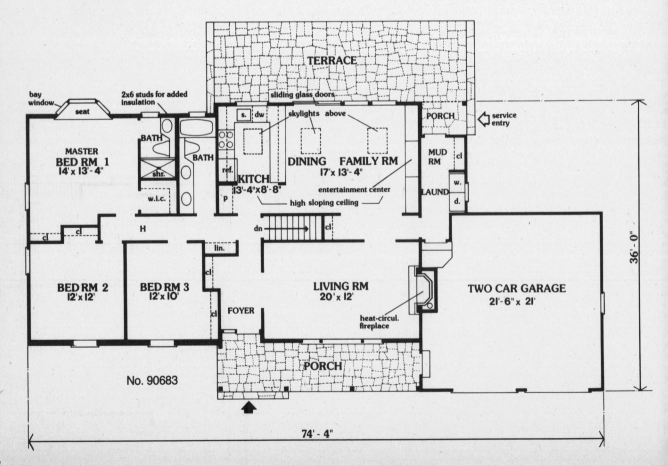

Year Round Retreat

No. 90613

This compact home is a bargain to build and designed to save on energy bills. Large glass areas face south, and the dramatic sloping ceiling of the living room allows heat from the wood-burning stove to rise into the upstairs bedrooms through high louvers on the inside wall. In hot weather, just open the windows on both floors for cooling air circulation. Sliding glass doors in the kitchen and living rooms open to the deck for outdoor dining or relaxation. One bedroom and a full bath complete the first floor. A stair off the foyer ends in a balcony with a commanding view of the living room. Two spacious bedrooms are separated by a full bath.

First floor — 917 sq. ft.
Second floor — 465 sq. ft.
(optional slab construction available)

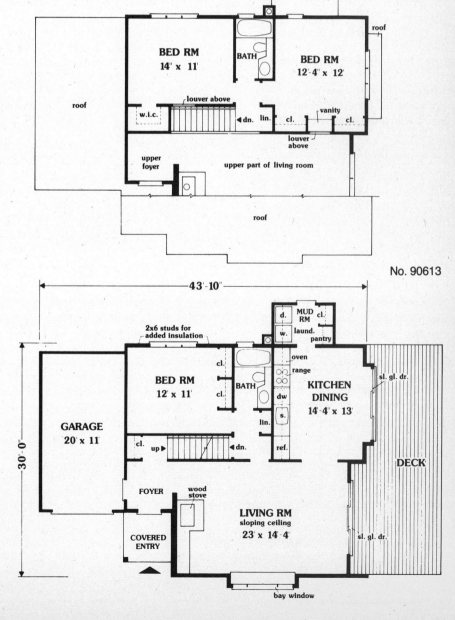

No. 90613

BED RM 14' x 11'
BATH
BED RM 12'-4" x 12'
roof
roof
roof
w.i.c.
louver above
dn. lin. cl. vanity cl.
louver above
upper foyer
upper part of living room
roof

43'-10"
30'-0"

2x6 studs for added insulation
d. MUD RM cl.
w. laund. pantry
oven
range
GARAGE 20' x 11'
BED RM 12' x 11'
cl.
BATH
dw
KITCHEN DINING 14'-4" x 13'
sl. gl. dr.
cl.
s.
lin.
cl. up dn. ref.
DECK
FOYER
wood stove
LIVING RM sloping ceiling 23' x 14'-4"
sl. gl. dr.
COVERED ENTRY
bay window

The Best of Both Worlds

No. 90551

Here's a home that combines centuries-old traditional styling with a touch of contemporary class. Elements of long-ago include the angular living room bay, the central staircase, and the glowing warmth of the family room fireplace. But, the vaulted space of the curving living room that opens to the formal dining room, the convenience of a first-floor master suite with a step-in shower, and the lofty view of the family room and breakfast nook from the second-floor vantage point are thoroughly modern. Three bedrooms and a full bath upstairs mean you'll have room to grow, so you can enjoy this wonderful home for many, many years.

First floor — 1,457 sq. ft.
Second floor — 747 sq. ft.
Garage — 2-car

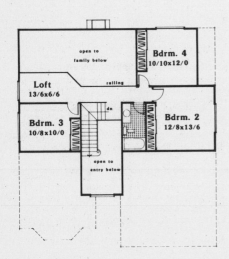

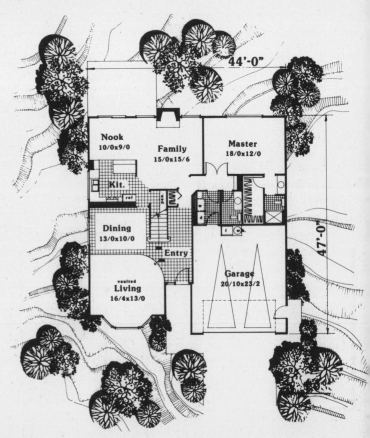

No. 90551

Cathedral Ceiling with Studio

No. 90420

This rustic-contemporary modified A-Frame design combines a high cathedral ceiling over a sunken living room with a large studio over the two rear bedrooms. The isolated master suite features a walk-in closet and compartmentalized bath with double vanity and linen closet.

The two rear bedrooms include ample closet space and share a unique bath-and-a-half arrangement. On one side of the U-shaped kitchen and breakfast nook is the formal dining room which is separated from the entry by the planter. On the other side is a utility room which can be entered from either the kitchen or garage. The exterior features a massive stone fireplace, large glass areas and a combination of vertical wood siding and stone.

First floor — 2,213 sq. ft.
Second floor — 260 sq. ft.
Basement — 2,213 sq. ft.
Garage — 422 sq. ft.

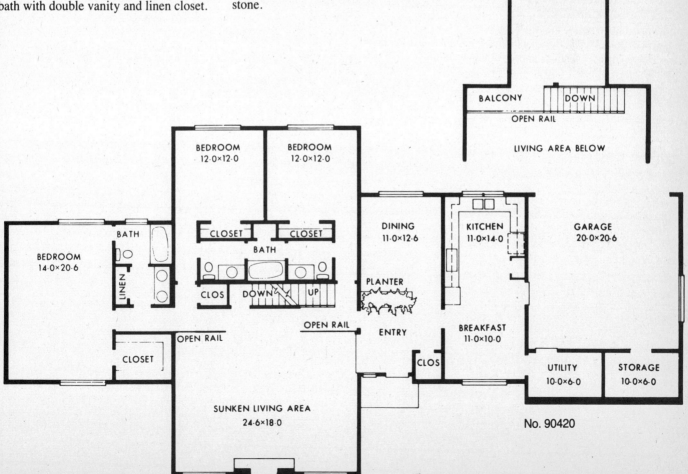

Build this House in a Beautiful Spot

No. 90672

This family home combines the charm of an early American Saltbox with contemporary drama. With a rear wall that's almost entirely glass and soaring ceilings pierced by skylights, active areas on the first floor unite with a full-length deck and backyard for an incredible outdoor feeling. But, beauty doesn't mean convenience has to be compromised. Look at the efficient galley kitchen, the adjoining pantry right by the rear entry, and the first-floor master bedroom served by a full bath. Survey the living areas below from the second floor balcony that opens to two bedrooms and another full bath.

First floor — 1,042 sq. ft.
Second floor — 519 sq. ft.
Mud/laundry room — 58 sq. ft.
Basement — 1,000 sq. ft.
Garage — 234 sq. ft.

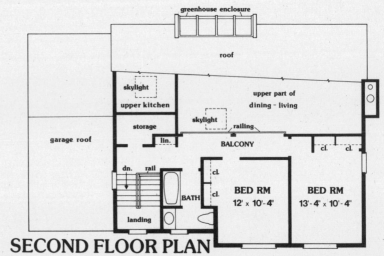

SECOND FLOOR PLAN

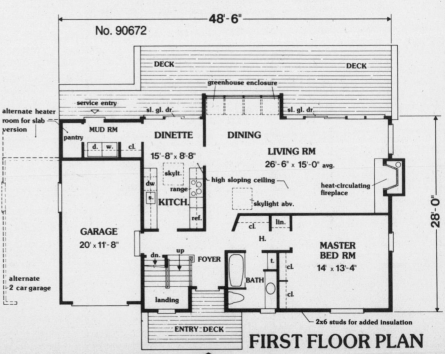

FIRST FLOOR PLAN

Country Living in Any Neighborhood

No. 90436

Put out the rocking chairs and watch the world go by from the covered porch of this appealing family classic. Inside, a cozy atmosphere pervades living spaces, from the fireplace in the expansive family room to the bay windows in both dining and breakfast rooms. You'll appreciate the strategic location of the large, well-appointed kitchen, just steps away from eating areas. When the alarm goes off, you'll also love the first-floor placement of the master suite. And, look at the double-vanitied bath that wraps around his and hers closets in this luxurious retreat. Both upstairs bedrooms feature dormer nooks, and private dressing rooms with an adjoining bath.

First floor — 1,477 sq. ft.
Second floor — 704 sq. ft.
Basement — 1,374 sq. ft.
Garage — 2-car

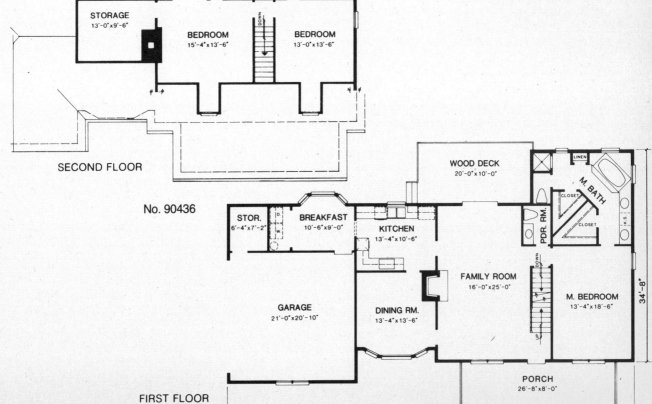

Fireplace Dominates Rustic Design

No. 90409

The ample porch of this charming home deserves a rocking chair, and there's room for two or three if you'd like. The front entry opens to an expansive great room with a soaring cathedral ceiling. Flanked by the master suite and two bedrooms with a full bath, the great room is separated from formal dining by a massive fireplace. The convenient galley kitchen adjoins a sunny breakfast nook, perfect for informal family dining.

Living area — 1,670 sq. ft.

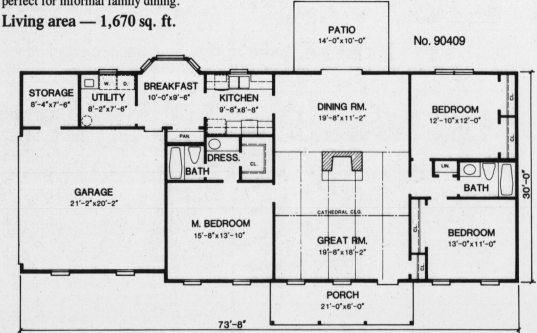

Soaring Roof Lines Hint at Dramatic Interior

No. 91405
From the vaulted living room to the bayed master bath, every room in this three-bedroom beauty features interesting

angles. The spacious, living-dining room arrangement at the front of the house is steps away from the kitchen. Three corner windows lend a greenhouse feeling to this well-appointed room, which opens to the informal dining bay and fireplaced family room. An elegant, U-shaped staircase leads to sleeping areas, tucked upstairs for a quiet atmosphere. There are

lots of options in this intriguing home, including a bonus room over the garage if you need the space. Specify a crawl-space or basement when ordering this plan.

First floor — 1,162 sq. ft.
Second floor — 807 sq. ft.
Garage — 446 sq. ft.

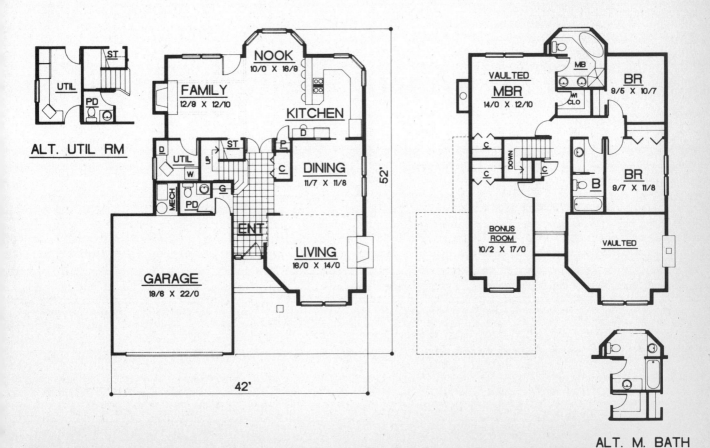

Greenhouse Brightens Compact Home

No. 20053

The kitchen features breakfast space, a built-in desk, pantry and a compact laundry area. Also on the first floor is the master bedroom with its private, five-piece bath. Both the entry foyer and the living room are open to the second floor creating a bridge between the two second floor bedrooms. In addition to the second floor's two bedrooms, full bath and linen closet, there is access to a large storage area under the eaves.

First floor — 1,088 sq. ft.
Second floor — 451 sq. ft.
Greenhouse — 72 sq. ft.
Garage — 473 sq. ft.

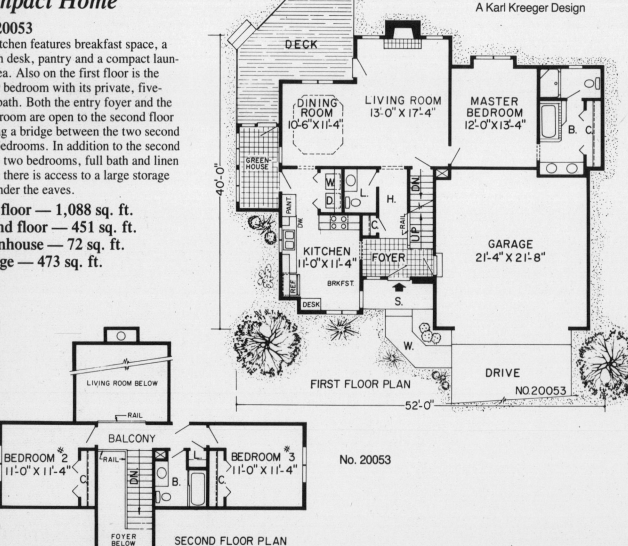

A Karl Kreeger Design

DECK

DINING ROOM 10'-6" X 11'-4"

GREEN-HOUSE

LIVING ROOM 13'-0" X 17'-4"

MASTER BEDROOM 12'-0" X 13'-4"

B. C.

PANT

W D L H.

DW C

REF

KITCHEN 11'-0" X 11'-4"

BRKFST.

FOYER

DESK

UP RAIL DN

GARAGE 21'-4" X 21'-8"

S.

W.

DRIVE

40'-0"

FIRST FLOOR PLAN

NO. 20053

52'-0"

LIVING ROOM BELOW

RAIL

BALCONY

RAIL

BEDROOM #2 11'-0" X 11'-4"

C

DN

L.

B.

BEDROOM #3 11'-0" X 11'-4"

C.

No. 20053

FOYER BELOW

SECOND FLOOR PLAN

Fireplace Wall Provides Warmth, Divides Active Areas

No. 90381

Appealing angles and well-placed windows set this distinctive three-bedroom beauty apart from the average, two-story home. The energy-saving vestibule entry opens to a central hallway dominated by an impressive staircase. The angular kitchen to the right, flooded with sun from oversized windows, features pass-through convenience to the adjoining dining room. Step back to the vaulted living room. Sliders unite this dramatic room with a rear deck. You'll appreciate the first-floor master suite, which includes a two-part bath for early morning convenience. Upstairs, a sunny mini-loft links the bedrooms and full bath, providing a bird's eye view of the living room below.

First floor — 1,189 sq. ft.
Second floor — 550 sq. ft.
Garage — 2-car

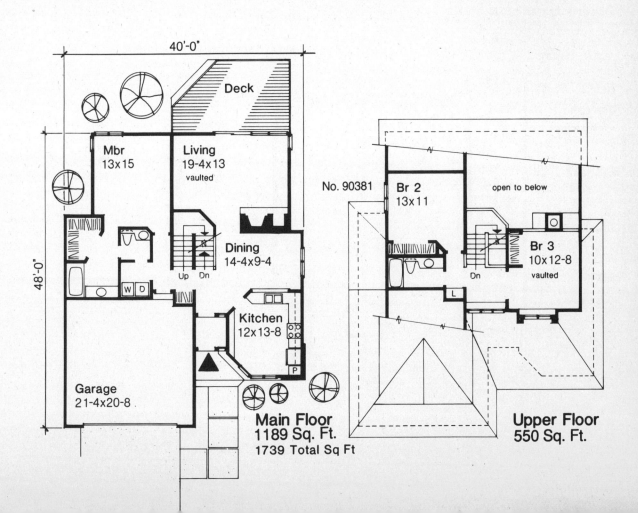

Main Floor
1189 Sq. Ft.
1739 Total Sq Ft

Upper Floor
550 Sq. Ft.

Contemporary Design Features Sunken Living Room

No. 26112

Wood adds its warmth to the contemporary features of this passive solar design. Generous use of southern glass doors and windows, an air-lock entry, skylights and a living room fireplace reduce energy needs. R-26 insulation is used for floors and sloping ceilings. Decking rims the front of the home and gives access through sliding glass doors to a bedroom-den area and living room. The dining room lies up several steps from the living room and is separated from it by a half wall. The dining room flows into the kitchen through an eating bar. A second floor landing balcony overlooks the living room. Two bedrooms, one with its own private deck, and a full bath finish the second level.

First floor — 911 sq. ft.
Second floor — 576 sq. ft.
Basement — 911 sq. ft.

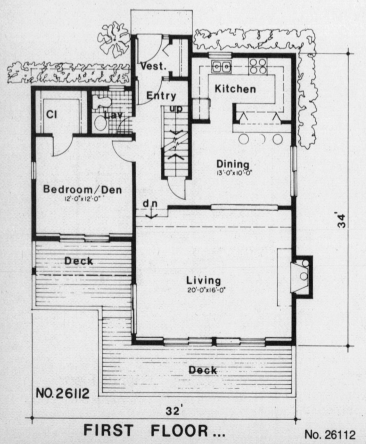

NO. 26112

32'

FIRST FLOOR ...

No. 26112

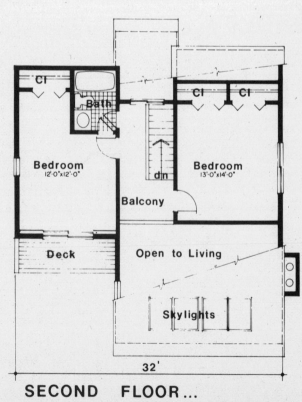

32'

SECOND FLOOR ...

Delightful Colonial Design

No. 90138

A quick study of this traditional colonial design will highlight many features desired by homemakers. The exterior of this plan exhibits traditional double-hung windows and horizontal siding all around the house. The first floor living room is completely separated from all other rooms for formal entertaining. The informal family room is at the rear of the house and features a wood-burning fireplace. Sliding glass doors in the breakfast area lead to an outdoor patio which shares its view with the kitchen. A large pantry is located within the kitchen while the laundry facilities are close by. The second floor features four bedrooms and two full baths.

First floor — 1,152 sq. ft.
Second floor — 1,152 sq. ft.

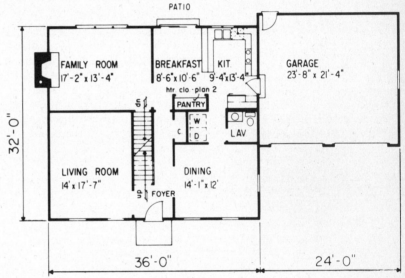

FIRST FLOOR

No. 90138

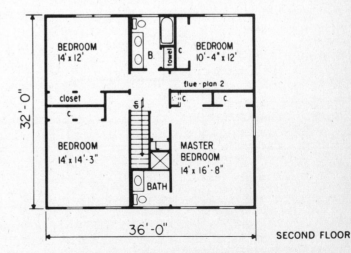

SECOND FLOOR

Attractive and Affordable

No. 90387

Plants and people alike will love the sunny atmosphere of this cheerful, three-bedroom home. The raised entry, dominated by a stairway to the second floor, overlooks the sunken living room. Wraparound windows and soaring ceilings add dramatic impact to this spacious area, warmed by the cozy glow of a fireplace. Look at the country kitchen at the rear of the house, with its greenhouse window, pass-through convenience to the formal dining room, and sliders to the rear deck. Upstairs, bedrooms are arranged for convenience. The full bath features two-way access: from the hallway, and through a private entrance in the master bedroom. Notice the beautiful alcove created by the half-round window in the front bedroom.

First floor — 713 sq. ft.
Second floor — 691 sq. ft.
Garage — 2-car

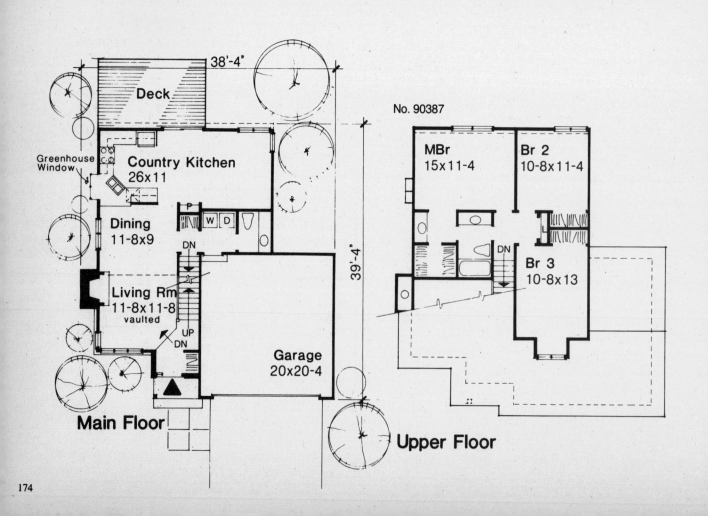

Contemporary Ranch Design

No. 26740

Sloping cathedral ceilings are found throughout the entirety of this home. A kitchen holds the central spot in the floor plan. It is partially open to a great hall with firebox and deck access on one side, daylight room lit by ceiling glass and full length windows on another, and entryway hallway on a third. The daylight room leads out onto a unique double deck. Bedrooms lie to the outside of the plan. Two smaller bedrooms at the rear share a full bath. The more secluded master bedroom at the front has its own full bath and access to a private deck.

Living area — 1,512 sq. ft.
Garage — 478 sq. ft.

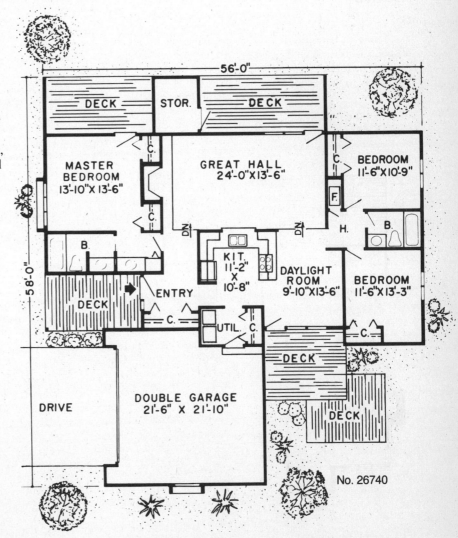

No. 26740

Dramatic Shape and Features

No. 10274

If your lot is the right shape, build this magnificent plan. A dramatically positioned fireplace forms the focus of a contemporary living area. Kitchen, dining, and living spaces are fashioned into a huge central room that flows from the heart of the home through sliding doors to the dramatic deck. The many flexible decorating options, such as screens and room dividers or conversational groupings, are impressive. A huge master bedroom and two roomy bedrooms are tucked in a wing away from the main area for privacy.

First floor — 1,783 sq. ft.
Garage — 576 sq. ft.

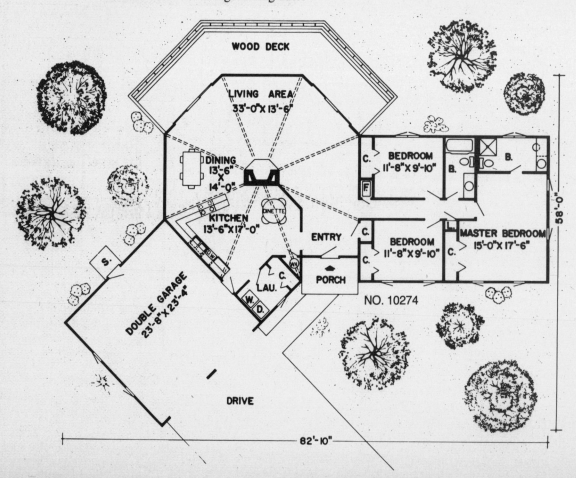

Open Space Characterizes Compact Plan

No. 90386

A vaulted entry, lit from above by a double window, provides an impressive introduction to this distinctive family home. The excitement continues as you proceed into the soaring living room and adjoining dining room, set apart from family areas for elegant entertaining. At the rear of the house, the country kitchen features a cozy fireplace, a bay window just perfect for your kitchen table, and access to a rear deck. The natural light present in the entry illuminates the stairwell through a half-round window that's beautiful from both interior and exterior perspectives. Three bedrooms and two full baths include the dramatically vaulted master suite at the rear of the house.

First floor — 928 sq. ft.
Second floor — 907 sq. ft.
Garage — 2-car

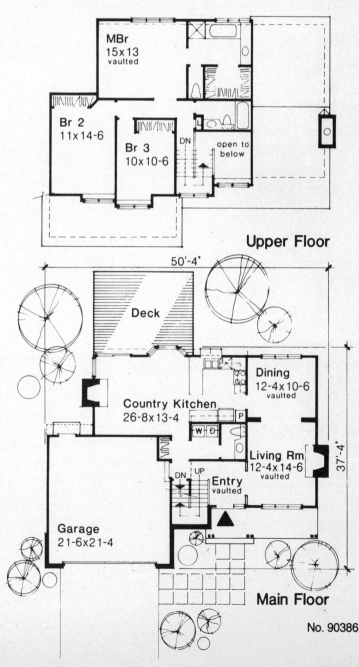

Upper Floor

MBr 15x13 vaulted
Br 2 11x14-6
Br 3 10x10-6
DN
open to below

Main Floor

Deck
Dining 12-4x10-6 vaulted
Country Kitchen 26-8x13-4
Living Rm 12-4x14-6 vaulted
Entry vaulted
Garage 21-6x21-4
50'-4"
37'-4"

No. 90386

Compact, Contemporary Design

No. 90101

This compact home is designed so that you can finish each section as needed or all at the beginning. This type of plan is perfect for a flexible budget or a growing family. Ideal for a narrow lot, this home features a vaulted ceiling above the open living room which blends into the dining area adjacent to the efficiently designed kitchen. The first floor also includes two bedrooms and a roomy bath. Second floor bedrooms and bath may be completed at a future date, as may the optional garage.

First floor — 988 sq. ft.
Second floor — 520 sq. ft.

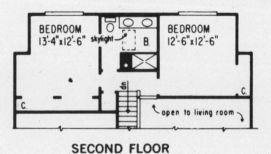

BEDROOM 13'-4"x12'-6" skylight   B.   BEDROOM 12'-6"x12'-6"

C.   C.

← open to living room →

SECOND FLOOR

38'-0"
11.58m

PATIO

20'-0"
6.1m

BEDROOM 10'x10'   B.   DINING 10'x10'-4"   KITCHEN 8'x10'

28'-0"
8.53m

C.   2nd floor line

MASTER BEDROOM 13'-4"x12'-6"   C.   LIVING ROOM 17'-5"x15'   OPTIONAL GARAGE 19'-8"x23'-4"

C.

FIRST FLOOR PLAN 1 WITH BASEMENT
No. 90101

Contemporary Classic on Three Levels

No. 20081

You'll find wonderfully shaped rooms, soaring ceilings, and an abundance of windows in this cheery contemporary home. Sharing the first level with the foyer, the master suite features a towering half-round window and private bath with double sinks. Up a few stairs, active areas are arranged for convenience. Notice the location of the kitchen, just steps away from formal and informal dining rooms. The living room is warmed by a fireplace, and boasts easy access to an outdoor deck. Two more bedrooms, tucked upstairs in a quiet spot, are connected by a balcony that overlooks the foyer.

First floor — 1,374 sq. ft.
Second floor — 489 sq. ft.
Basement — 845 sq. ft.
Garage — 484 sq. ft.

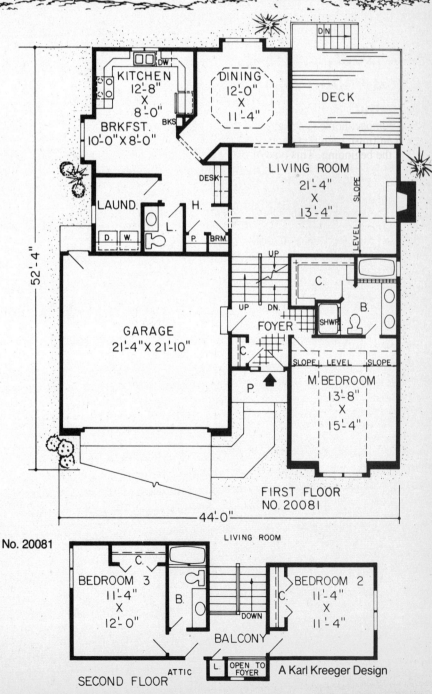

FIRST FLOOR
NO. 20081

SECOND FLOOR

A Karl Kreeger Design

House with a View

No. 90418

Modest in appearance this vacation home offers open living area. The two-level home has two bedrooms and a bath located on the upper level and another bedroom and bath on the lower level. A kitchen and utility room are located off the living-dining area.

First floor — 1,304 sq. ft.
Second floor — 303 sq. ft.

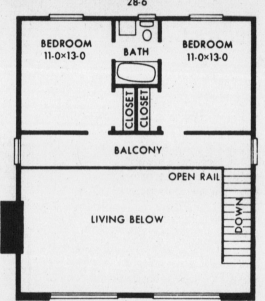

28-6

BEDROOM
11-0×13-0

BATH

BEDROOM
11-0×13-0

CLOSET CLOSET

BALCONY

OPEN RAIL

LIVING BELOW

DOWN

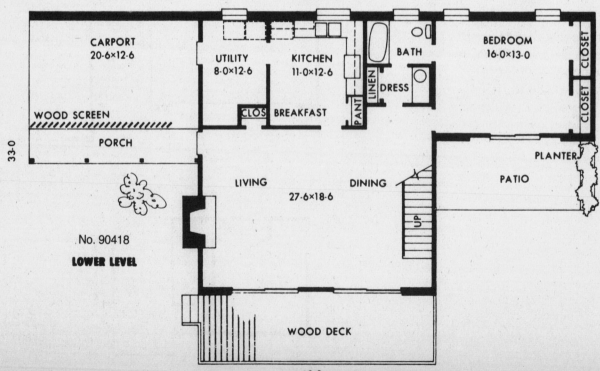

CARPORT
20-6×12-6

UTILITY
8-0×12-6

KITCHEN
11-0×12-6

BATH

BEDROOM
16-0×13-0

CLOSET

CLOSET

LINEN

DRESS

PANT

WOOD SCREEN

CLOS. BREAKFAST

33-0

PORCH

LIVING
27-6×18-6

DINING

UP

PATIO

PLANTER

No. 90418
LOWER LEVEL

WOOD DECK

68-0

Small but Spacious

No. 91312

Remove unnecessary hallways and walls,
add an abundant supply of windows, and
you've got a compact contemporary with
a wide-open feeling. Stand in the spacious entry, dominated by an open staircase. To the left, a fireplaced family
room adjoins a bay-windowed breakfast
nook off the kitchen. To the right, an elegant, sunken living room, featuring a
corner window arrangement and cheerful
bay, is steps away from the formal dining
room. You'll love the compact kitchen
at the rear of the house, convenient to
both eating areas. Upstairs, the two front
bedrooms share a spectacular, arched
window and a double-vanitied full bath.
The rear master suite enjoys a private
bath and sunny bay sitting nook.

First floor — 879 sq. ft.
Second floor — 746 sq. ft.

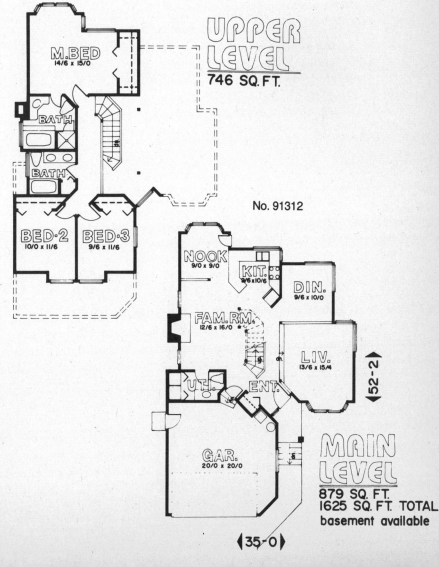

UPPER LEVEL
746 SQ. FT.

M.BED
14/6 x 15/0

BATH

BATH

BED-2
10/0 x 11/6

BED-3
9/6 x 11/6

No. 91312

NOOK
9/0 x 9/0

KIT.
9/6 x 10/6

DIN.
9/6 x 10/0

FAM.RM.
12/6 x 16/0

LIV.
13/6 x 15/4

UT.

ENT.

52-2

GAR.
20/0 x 20/0

MAIN LEVEL
879 SQ. FT.
1625 SQ. FT. TOTAL
basement available

35-0

Mud Room Separates Garage and Kitchen

No. 9812

Gardening and woodworking tools will find a home in the storage closet of the useful mud room in this rustic detailed ranch. Besides incorporating a laundry area, the mud room will prove invaluable as a place for removing snowy boots and draining wet umbrellas. The family room appendages the open kitchen and flows outward to the stone terrace. The master bedroom is furnished with a private bath and protruding closet space, and the living room retains a formality by being situated to the left of the entryway.

First floor — 1,396 sq. ft.
Basement — 1,396 sq. ft.
Garage — 484 sq. ft.

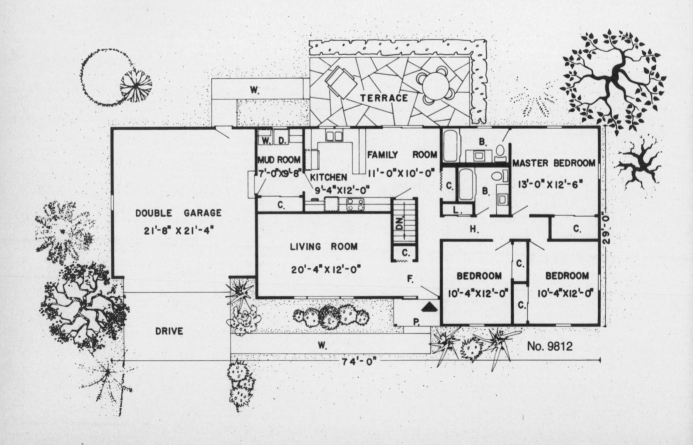

Porch Adds Shelter, Classic Appeal

No. 90217

Whether you need three or four bedrooms, this traditional plan boasts a versatile character that can change to fit your lifestyle. Main living areas open off a central entry dominated by a handsome staircase. Entertain in the formal living and dining rooms, which flow together in a spacious, L-shaped arrangement. You'll find the same open ambiance in the family area off the kitchen, which includes a sunny breakfast nook overlooking a sunken, fireplaced family room with a rustic beamed ceiling and sliders to the rear terrace. Two full baths serve the bedrooms upstairs, completing this compact family home.

First floor — 990 sq. ft.
Second floor — 728 sq. ft.
Garage — 2-car

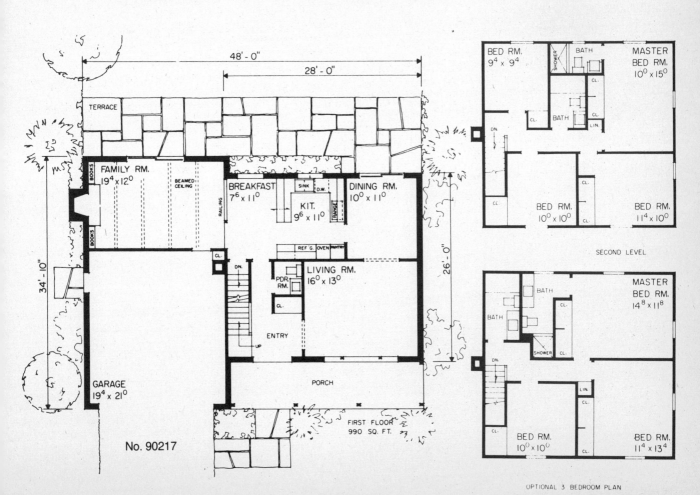

Appealing Contemporary Design

No. 90366

The story-and-a-half house provides an opportunity to combine old-fashioned value with contemporary design appeal. This house looks and lives contemporary with its dramatic entrance and vaulted ceiling space, its garden kitchen, its flexible, open living-dining-kitchen area and its generous master bedroom dressing closet. Note, also, the modern convenience of the mudroom-laundry entrance. Yet with a door to block hallway access, the upstairs can be left unfinished to reduce initial cash requirements. The two bedrooms and bath with an optional operable skylight can be a do-it-yourself project to be finished later. If built without a basement, mechanical equipment can be placed under the stairs.

Main living area — 1,549 sq. ft.

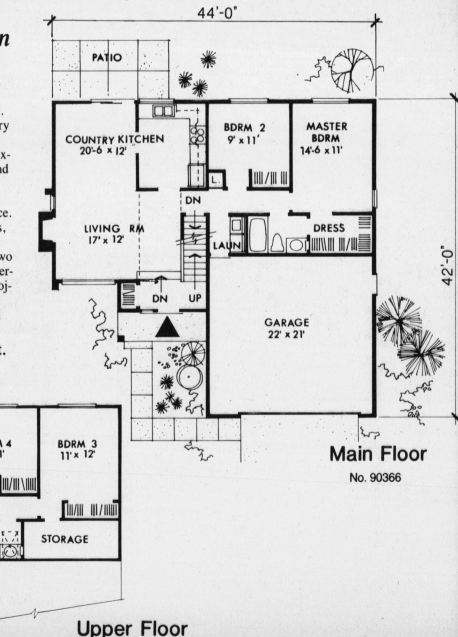

Main Floor

No. 90366

Upper Floor

Breathtaking Views — Inside and Out

No. 91224

The luxury of a skylit tub and a private balcony in your own fireplaced master suite should be enough to convince you that this is your dream house. But, this three-bedroom gem is loaded with convenient features, too. Notice the placement of the island kitchen between formal and informal dining rooms. You'll appreciate the handy garage entry when your arms are loaded with groceries. And, with a powder room on the first floor, and a wetbar steps away, visiting guests won't have to go too far from the comfort of the roaring fire in your spacious living room.

First floor — 997 sq. ft.
Second floor — 1,059 sq. ft.
Garage — 506 sq. ft.

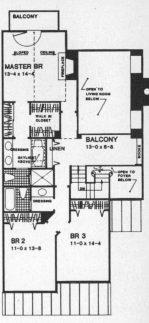

LIVING RM

BRKFST · **FOYER**

BALCONY ABOVE · WET BAR

FRENCH DOORS · BALCONY ABOVE · COATS

HVAC CHASE · HIGH FLAT CEILING

GAR STOR · DN

GARAGE · **PORCH**

OPTIONAL BASEMENT PLAN

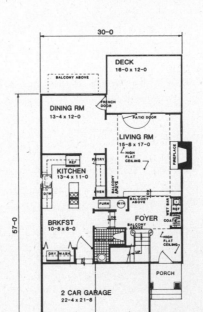

30-0

57-0

DECK
16-0 x 12-0

BALCONY ABOVE

FRENCH DOOR

DINING RM
13-4 x 12-0

PATIO DOOR

LIVING RM
15-8 x 17-0
HIGH FLAT CEILING

FIREPLACE

REF · PANTRY

KITCHEN
13-4 x 11-0

OVEN · BALCONY ABOVE

FURN · WTH

D/W

BRKFST
10-8 x 8-0

WET BAR · REF

FOYER
BALCONY ABOVE · COAT

DRY · WASH

HIGH FLAT CEILING · UP

2 CAR GARAGE
22-4 x 21-8

PORCH

FIRST FLOOR PLAN

BALCONY

SLOPED · CEILING · FIREPLACE

MASTER BR
13-4 x 14-4

OPEN TO LIVING ROOM BELOW

WALK IN CLOSET

DRESSING · LINEN

BALCONY
13-0 x 6-8

SKYLIGHT ABOVE · DRESSING

OPEN TO FOYER BELOW

DN

BR 2
11-0 x 13-8

BR 3
11-0 x 14-4

SECOND FLOOR PLAN

No. 91224

No materials list available

Angular Fireplace Adds Interest

No. 20125

With it spacious, garage-level shop area, this attractive brick and wood-sided classic is the perfect abode for the home hobbyist. The main floor active space surrounds a central staircase. Formal areas off the foyer at the front of the house are ideal for entertaining. Your guests will enjoy the cozy atmosphere of the fireplaced living room, and the quiet elegance of the formal dining room. The kitchen, breakfast bay and utility room share a backyard view, and access to the rear deck. With its raised tub, double vanities, and step-in shower, the first-floor master suite is a private, yet convenient retreat you're sure to appreciate. Two bedrooms upstairs share another full bath.

First floor — 1,340 sq. ft.
Second floor — 455 sq. ft.
Basement — 347 sq. ft.
Garage — 979 sq. ft.

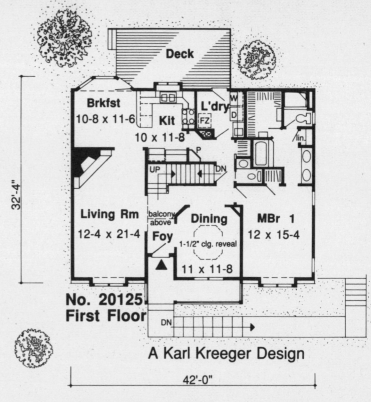

No. 20125
First Floor

A Karl Kreeger Design

No. 20125

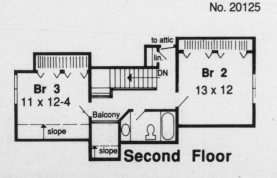

Second Floor

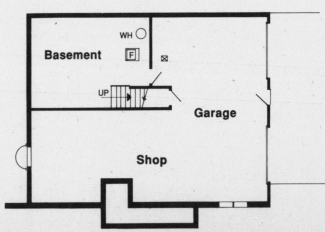

Colonial Ranch Style, Enriched Interior

No. 9864

Endowed with the trimmings of a traditional colonial, this three-bedroom ranch is doubly attractive. The master bedroom is complete with a full bath, walk-in closet and spacious dressing area. Warmed by a wood-burning fireplace, the living room spills onto a large redwood deck via a sliding glass door. A functional kitchen is separated from the family room by a cooking peninsula. A utility room and hobby shop edge the double garage.

First floor — 1,612 sq. ft.
Basement — 1,612 sq. ft.
Garage, utility room and storage — 660 sq. ft.

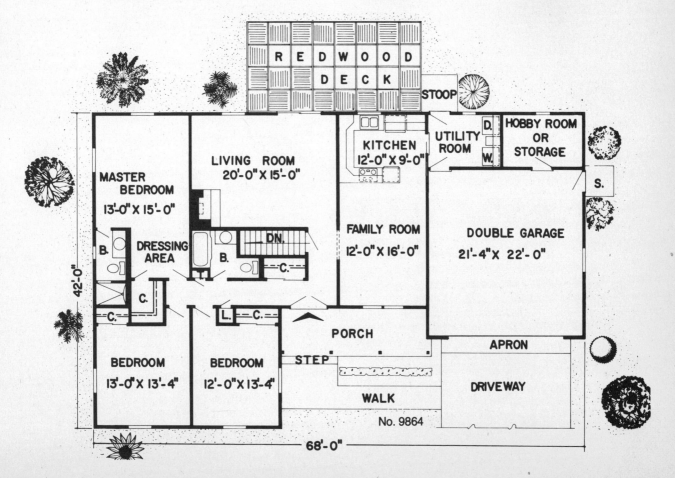

REDWOOD DECK

STOOP

MASTER BEDROOM 13'-0" X 15'-0"

LIVING ROOM 20'-0" X 15'-0"

KITCHEN 12'-0" X 9'-0"

UTILITY ROOM

D. W.

HOBBY ROOM OR STORAGE

S.

DRESSING AREA

DN.

FAMILY ROOM 12'-0" X 16'-0"

DOUBLE GARAGE 21'-4" X 22'-0"

B.

B.

C.

C.

C.

42'-0"

BEDROOM 13'-0" X 13'-4"

BEDROOM 12'-0" X 13'-4"

L. C.

STEP

PORCH

APRON

WALK

DRIVEWAY

No. 9864

68'-0"

Order Your Blueprints Now!

How Many Sets of Plans Will You Need?

Experience shows that the **Standard 8-Set Construction Package** is best. You'll speed every step of construction and avoid costly building errors by ordering enough sets to go around. And, usually everyone wants their own set. Consider your lending institution, general contractor and all of his subcontractors; foundation; framing; electrical; plumbing; heating/air conditioning; drywall; and finish carpenters – as well as a set for you.

Minimum 5-Set Construction Package gives an efficient planner a choice. Although eight sets relieves you of worry about sets being lost or ruined on the job, you can carefully hand sets down as work progresses and might have enough copies to go around with the five set package.

One Complete Set of Blueprints lets you study the blueprints, so you can plan your dream home. But, keep in mind . . . One set is never enough for actually building your home.

Here's What You Get!

Our accurate and complete blueprints contain everything you need to begin building your dream home:

- Front, rear, and both side views of the house (elevations)
- Floor plans for all levels
- Roof plan
- Foundation plan
- Universal Plot plan
- Typical wall sections (sectional slices throughout the home)
- Kitchen and bathroom cabinet details
- Fireplace details (where applicable)
- Stair details (where applicable)
- Locations of electrical fixtures and components
- Specifications and contract form
- Energy Conservation Specifications Guide

Please note: All plans are drawn to conform with one or more of the industry's major national building standards. However, local building codes may differ from national standards. We recommend that you check with your local building officials.

Remember to Order a Materials List!

Our materials list for your home plan will help you save money! This helpful list is available at a small additional charge and gives the quantity, dimensions and specifications for all major materials needed to build your home (small hardware like nails, screws, etc. are omitted). With this valuable list, you'll get faster and more accurate bids from your contractors and building suppliers. In addition, you'll avoid paying for unnecessary materials and waste.

Materials lists are available for all home plans except where otherwise indicated, but can only be ordered along with a set of home plans. **Please Note:** Due to differences in local building codes, regional requirements and builder preferences . . . electrical, plumbing, and heating/air conditioning equipment requirements are not provided as part of the material list.

Discover Reverse Plans at no extra charge!

You may find that a particular house would suit your taste or fit your lot better if it were "reversed." A reverse plan turns the design end-for-end. That is, if the garage is shown on the left side and the bedrooms on the right, the reverse plan will place the garage on the right side and the bedrooms on the left. To see quickly how a design will look in reverse, hold your book up to a mirror.

If you want to build your Garlinghouse Home in reverse, then order your plans reversed. You'll receive one mirror-image, reversed set of plans (with "backwards" lettering and dimensions) as a master guide for you and your builder. The remaining sets in your order are then sent as shown in our publication for ease in reading the lettering and dimensions. These "as shown" sets will all be marked "REVERSED" with a special stamp to eliminate confusion on the job site. **Reverse plans are available only on multiple set orders.**

Modify Your Garlinghouse Home Plan!

Your custom dream home can be as wonderful as you want. Easy modifications, such as minor non-structural changes and simple building material substitutions, can be made by any competent builder without the need for blueprint revisions.

However, if you are considering making major changes to your design, we strongly recommend that you seek the services of an architect or professional designer. Even these expensive professional services will cost less with our complete, detailed blueprints as a starting point.

Reproducible Mylars Make Plan Modifications Easier!

Ask about our Reproducible Mylars for your home design. They're inexpensive and provide a design professional with a way to make custom changes directly to our home plans and then print as many copies as you need of the modified design. It's a perfect way to create a truly custom home! Prices range from $340 to $415 plus mailing charges. **Call 1-800-235-5700 to find out more about our Reproducible Mylars.** Please Note: Reproducible mylars are not available for plans numbered 90,000 and above, or for plans numbered 19,000 through 19,999.

PRICE SCHEDULE

One Complete Set of Blueprints	$125.00
Minimum Construction Package (5 Sets)	$170.00
Standard Construction Package (8 Sets)	$200.00
Each Additional Set Ordered With One of the Above Packages	$20.00
Materials List (with plan order only)	$15.00

Prices are subject to change without notice

Important Shipping Information

Your order receives our immediate attention! However, please allow 10 working days from our receipt of your order for normal UPS delivery. You can call in your credit card order TOLL FREE and avoid the additional mail delay for your order to reach us.

Note that UPS will deliver **only** to street addresses and rural route delivery boxes and **not** to Post Office Box Numbers. Please print your complete street address. If no one is home during the day, you may use your work address to insure prompt delivery.

We **MUST** ship First Class Mail to Alaska or Hawaii, APO, FPO, or a Post Office Box. Please note the higher cost for First Class Mail.

Domestic Shipping

UPS Ground Service	**$6.00**
First Class Mail	**$7.75**
Express Delivery Service	Call for details 1-800-235-5700

International Orders & Shipping

Mexico & Other Countries:

If you are ordering from outside the United States, please note that your check, money order, or international money transfer **must be payable in U.S. currency.**

We ship all international orders via Air Parcel Post for delivery (surface mail is extremely slow). Please refer to the schedule below for the mailing charge on your order and substitute this amount for the usual mailing charges for domestic orders.

Canadian Orders & Shipping:

Our plan design affiliate in Kitchener, Ontario will help our Canadian friends avoid the delays and duties associated with shipments from the U.S. Moreover, our affiliate is familiar with the building requirements in your community and country.

Please submit all Canadian plan orders to:

The Garlinghouse Co., Inc.
20 Cedar St. N., Kitchener, Ont. N2H 2W8
Phone 519-743-4169 • Fax 519-743-1282

When sending Canadian funds, please add 20% to ALL prices shown. Ontario residents also add 8% P.S.T.

International Shipping

	One Set	Multiple Sets
Canada	$5.75	$9.75
Mexico & Caribbean Nations	$16.50	$39.50
All other Nations	$18.50	$50.00

For Fastest Service...
ORDER TOLL FREE
1-800-235-5700

MasterCard *VISA*

Monday-Friday   8:00 am to 5:00 pm Eastern Time
Connecticut. Alaska. Hawaii & all foreign residents call 1-203-632-0500. Please have the following at your fingertips before you call:
1. Your credit card number
2. The plan number
3. The order code number

FAX: 1-203-632-0712

BLUEPRINT ORDER FORM

GARLINGHOUSE

Send your Check, Money Order or Credit Card information to:
The Garlinghouse Company
34 Industrial Park Place, P.O. Box 1717
Middletown, CT 06457

Order Code No.
H90A1

For Canadian Orders: The Garlinghouse Co. • 20 Cedar Street No. • Kitchener, Ontario N2H 2W8

PLAN NO._____

☐ as shown   ☐ reversed

QTY.

____ 1 Set Pkg. **($125.00)** . . . . . . = $ _____	
____ 5 Set Pkg. **($170.00)** . . . . . . = $ _____	
____ 8 Set Pkg. **($200.00)** . . . . . . = $ _____	
____ Additional Sets **($20.00 ea.)** . = $ _____	
____ Materials List **($15.00)** . . . . . = $ _____	
Shipping Charges (see charts) . . . . . = $ _____	
Subtotal . . . . = $ _____	
Sales Tax* . . . . = $ _____	

*Kansas residents add 5.25% sales tax
Connecticut residents add 8% sales tax

TOTAL AMOUNT ENCLOSED $ [   ]

Thank You for Your Order!

BILL TO:

Name_____
Please Print

Address_____

City & State_____ Zip_____

Phone (_____)_____

SHIP TO:

Name_____
Please Print

Address_____

City & State_____ Zip_____

Phone (_____)_____

METHOD OF PAYMENT: ☐ Check   ☐ Money Order

Charge to: ☐ Visa   ☐ MasterCard

Signature_____   Exp. Date _____/_____

Builder's Library

The books on this page were written with the professional home builder in mind. They are all comprehensive information sources for contractors or for those beginners who wish to build like contractors.

► **2600. Building Underground** This has been compiled on earth sheltered homes, built all over North America—homes that are spacious, attractive and comfortable in every way. These homes are more energy efficient than above ground houses. Physical security, low operating costs, and noise reduction further enhance their attractiveness. 304 pp.; 85 photos; 112 illus.; Rodale Press (paperback) **$14.95**

◄ **2518. Build Your Own Home** An authoritative guide on how to be your own general contractor. This book goes through the step-by-step process of building a house with special emphasis on the business aspects such as financing, scheduling, permits, insurance, and more. Furthermore, it gives you an understanding of what to expect out of your various subcontractors so that you can properly orchestrate their work. 112 pp.; Holland House (paperback) **$12.95**

from the Leading Publishers in the Do-It-Yourself Industry!!!

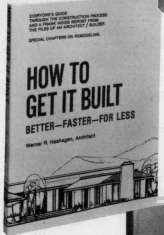

◄ **2596. How To Get It Built** No matter how small or how large your construction project is, building will be easier with this informative guidebook. This text was prepared for people involved in building on a non-professional basis. Guidelines have been carefully prepared to follow step-by-step construction-cost savings methods. Written by an architect/contractor, this book offers home construction owners the planning, construction and cost saving solutions to his own building needs. 238 pp.; over 300 illus.; (paperback) Hashagen **$18.00**

► **2508. Modern Plumbing** All aspects of plumbing installation, service, and repair are presented here in illustrated, easy-to-follow text. This book contains all the information needed for vocational competence, including the most up-to-date tools, materials, and practices. 300 pp.; over 700 illus.; Goodheart-Willcox (hardcover) **$19.96**

▲ **2620. Spas & Hot Tubs, Saunas & Home Gyms** Includes complete information on incorporating spas, hot tubs, saunas and exercise rooms into a home. Step-by-step installation instructions for spas, hot tubs, and saunas are included, along with a grid and templates for designing a home exercise room. Spa and hot tub maintenance and repairs is also covered. 160 pp.; Creative Homeowner Press (paperback) **$9.95**

▲ **2546. Blueprint Reading for Construction** This combination text and workbook shows and tells how to read residential, commercial, and light industrial prints. With an abundance of actual drawings from industry, you learn step by step about each component of a set of blueprints, including even cost estimating. 336 pp.; Goodheart-Willcox (spiral bound) **$21.28**

▲ **2570. Modern Masonry** Everything you will ever need to know about concrete, masonry, and brick, is included in this book. Forms construction, concrete reinforcement, proper foundation construction, and bricklaying are among the topics covered in step-by-step detail. An excellent all-round reference and guide. 256 pp.; 700 illus.; Goodheart-Willcox (hardcover) **$19.96**

▼ **2514. The Underground House Book** For anyone seriously interested in building and living in an underground home, this book tells it all. Aesthetic considerations, building codes, site planning, financing, insurance, planning and decorating considerations, maintenance costs, soil, excavation, landscaping, water considerations, humidity control, and specific case histories are among the many facets of underground living dealt with in this publication. 208 pp.; 140 illus.; Garden Way (paperback) **$10.95**

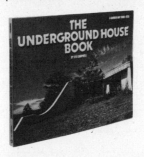

▼ **2504. Architecture, Residential Drawing and Design** An excellent text that explains all the fundamentals on how to create a complete set of construction drawings. Specific areas covered include proper design and planning considerations, foundation plans, floor plans, elevations, stairway details, electrical plans, plumbing plans, etc. 492 pp.; over 800 illus.; Goodheart-Willcox (hardcover) **$26.60**

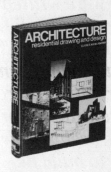

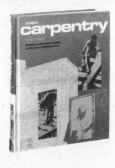

▲ **2510. Modern Carpentry** A complete guide to the "nuts and bolts" of building a home. This book explains all about building materials, framing, trim work, insulation, foundations, and much more. A valuable text and reference guide. 492 pp.; over 1400 illus.; Goodheart-Willcox (hardcover) **$25.20**

▲ **2506. House Wiring Simplified** This book teaches all the fundamentals of modern house wiring; shows how it's done with easy-to-understand drawings. A thorough guide to the materials and practices for safe, efficient installation of home electrical systems. 176 pp.; 384 illus.; Goodheart-Willcox (hardcover) **$10.00**

▼ **2618. Garages and Carports** Convert, expand and build for more living space. Site planning, complete plans, construction, wiring and more than 200 illustrations. 160 pp.; Creative Homeowner Press (paperback) **$8.95**

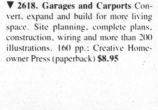

▼ **2622. Decks** Design and build your dream deck. Parts of a deck and materials used in construction are explained, including a list of essential tools. Step-by-step instructions on railing and step construction, overhead deck covers and deck maintenance are included. A clear explanation of the importance of outdoor lighting and how to design and install dramatic lighting is included. 160 pp.; Creative Homeowner Press (paperback) **$9.95**

▲ **2616. Adding Space Without Adding On** Expand your living space by transforming an attic or basement, adding a bathroom, or moving interior walls. Create closets and built-ins in space you never knew you had. Over 400 illustrations. 160 pp.; Creative Homeowner Press (paperback) **$8.95**

▲ **2556. Handbook of Doormaking, Windowmaking, and Staircasing** This publication is dedicated to the presentation of an almost lost art: Quality workmanship in homebuilding! This completely illustrated handbook offers clear, step-by-step instructions that will allow any carpenter (amateur or professional) to construct finely crafted doors, windows, and staircases. This book is meant for those who wish to take the time to build a quality home that will last. 256 pp.; 377 illus.; Sterling Publishing (paperback) **$8.95**

▼ **2611. Tile It Up! Plumb It Up!** Using the many illustrations and the easy steps included in this valuable book, you will be able to work just like the professionals. This book provides step-by-step instructions on plumbing and tiling, enabling the do-it-yourselfer to complete these projects with a minimum of time providing maximum results. 43 pp.; XS Books (paperback) **$6.95**

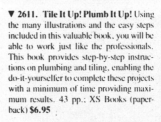

▼ **2516. Building Consultant** The new home buyer's bible to home construction. This encyclopedia of home building explains in comprehensive detail about all the various elements that go into a completed house. It enables you to deal with the construction of your new home in a meaningful way that will avoid costly errors, whether you use a contractor or build it yourself. 188 pp.; Holland House (paperback) **$12.95**

Builder's Library order form

Yes! send me the following books:

book order no.	price
_____	$ _____
_____	$ _____
_____	$ _____
_____	$ _____
_____	$ _____
_____	$ _____
_____	$ _____

Postage & handling (one book only) $ 1.75
Add 50¢ postage & handling
   for each additional book $ _____
Canada add $1.50 per book $ _____
Resident sales tax: Kansas (5.25%) $ _____
                     Connecticut (8%) $ _____
TOTAL ENCLOSED $ _____

No C.O.D. orders accepted; U.S. funds only.
prices subject to change without notice

My Shipping Address is:
(please print)

Name _____
Address _____
City _____
State _____ Zip _____

Send your order to:
(With check or money order enclosed)

**The Garlinghouse Company
34 Industrial Park Place
P.O. Box 1717
Middletown, Connecticut 06457**

For Faster Service . . .
CHARGE IT!   (203) 632-0500

☐ MasterCard   ☐ Visa

Card # |_|_|_|_|_|_|_|_|_|_|_| Exp. Date _____
Signature _____

▼ **2604. The Low Maintenance House** At last, an idea-packed book that will save you thousands of hours on home maintenance. It's an essential planning guide for anyone building a home. Discover new as well as time-tested techniques and products for cutting down the time, and slashing the money you spend to clean and repair your home . . . from roof to basement, from front yard to backyard garden. This book will earn its price, and your thanks, over and over again. 314 pp.; Rodale (hardback) **$19.95**

▲ **2605. Contracting Your Home** With over 150 illustrations, this guide offers many suggestions and ideas on contracting your own home. Many forms you can copy and re-use are provided, giving checklists and a glossary of terms used by the professionals, as well as all the necessary estimating forms. 279 pp.; Betterway Publications (paperback) **$18.95**

▼ **2614. Walls, Floors & Ceilings** Beautify your home's interior with any of 50 projects. Covers paint, wallpaper, paneling, and many remodeling ideas, including skylights. Over 500 photos and illustrations. 160 pp.; Creative Homeowner Press (paperback) **$8.95**

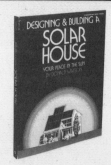

▲ **2542. Designing and Building a Solar House** Written by one of America's foremost authorities on solar architecture. It is a practical "how-to" guide that clearly demonstrates the most sensible ways to marry good house design with contemporary solar technology. Included is a thorough discussion of both "active" and "passive" solar systems, and even a listing of today's leading solar homes. 288 pp.; 400 illus.; Garden Way (paperback) **$15.95**

▼ **2610. The Backyard Builder** Here is a step-by-step guide for over 150 projects for the gardener and homeowner, accompanied by over 100 photos, 400 illustrations, materials lists and shopping guides. You are sure to find many useful, attractive projects that the entire family can help with. 656 pp.; Rodale (hardcover) **$21.95**

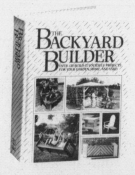

▲ **2606. Building Fences** With emphasis on function and style, this guide to a wide variety of fence-building is a solid how-to book. With easy-to-read instructions, and plenty of illustrations, this book is a must for the professional and the do-it-yourselfer. 188 pp.; Williamson Publishing (paperback) **$13.95**